URBANIZATION OVERSPEED
IN TROPICAL AFRICA, 1970—2000

To
MAGNOLIA

INU PRESS
Interuniversity Institute
CH-1211 Geneva-11, Switzerland

LC 84-52309
US Copyright Registration Number TXu 143-529
© 1986, Interuniversity Institute, Geneva

ISBN 2-88155-000-2

INU SOCIETAL RESEARCH SERIES
Dirk Pereboom, editor

Urbanization Overspeed in Tropical Africa, 1970–2000

Facts, Social Problems, and Policy

GUY ANKERL

INU PRESS
Interuniversity Institute,
CH–1211 Geneva–11, Switzerland

INU PRESS

By the same author

Experimental Sociology of Architecture: A Guide to Theory, Research, and Literature

Beyond Monopoly Capitalism and Monopoly Socialism: Distributive Justice in a Competitive Society

Sociologues Allemands: Etudes de Cas en Sociologie Historique et Non-historique avec le Dictionnaire de *"L'Ethique Protestante et l'Esprit du Capitalisme"* de Max Weber

L'Epanouissement de l'Homme dans les Perspectives de la Politique Economique: Concept de l'Investissement dans l'Homme comme Aspect de la Politique de Répartition

Urbanisation Rapide en Afrique Tropicale

CONTENTS

PREFACE   11

CHAPTER ONE
Review of Basic Data of Urbanization since Independence   15

State of urbanization in 1980   15
State of agglomerations in 1980   16
Trends of urbanizations between 1970–2000   17
Trends in urban concentration and in the development of agglomerations between 1970–2000   19
Activities and urbanization   24
1. Demographic sources of urban growth   25
2. Production and urbanization   27
3. Housing and urbanization   31

CHAPTER TWO
From Facts to Problems   35

The underprivileged   36
Underprivilege, an elusive phenomenon   38
The household in a transitional society   40
Differentiating rural and urban underprivileged   41
Measuring and monitoring the underprivileged's situation   43
Societal indicators   45
Indicators and the underprivileged in urban and rural areas   50
Public services in urban and rural areas   54
Housing   56
Food supply   58
Underemployment and the residual sector   60
Elderly, handicapped and children   61
Women   63

CHAPTER THREE
The Search for Solutions 69

Rural-urban migration: policy goals and measures for deceleration and redirection 69
Disincentives for migration 73
Social problem-solving by collective self-help 76
Social networks 77
Effective solidarity ties 80

CHAPTER FOUR
Summary of Policy Recommendations 87

SOURCES BIBLIOGRAPHY AND DATA 97

COMPLETE REFERENCE MAPS 113

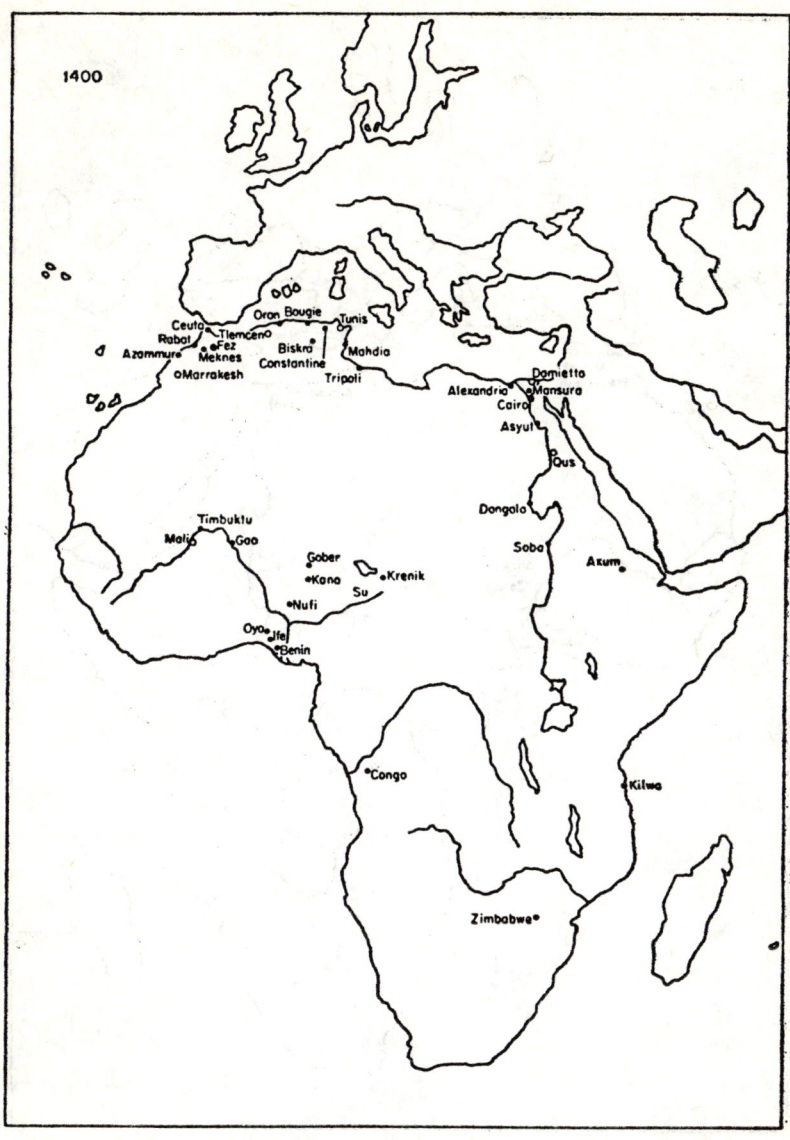

Cities over 20 000 inhabitants in 1400, viz. before Tropical Africa's eurocolonialization.

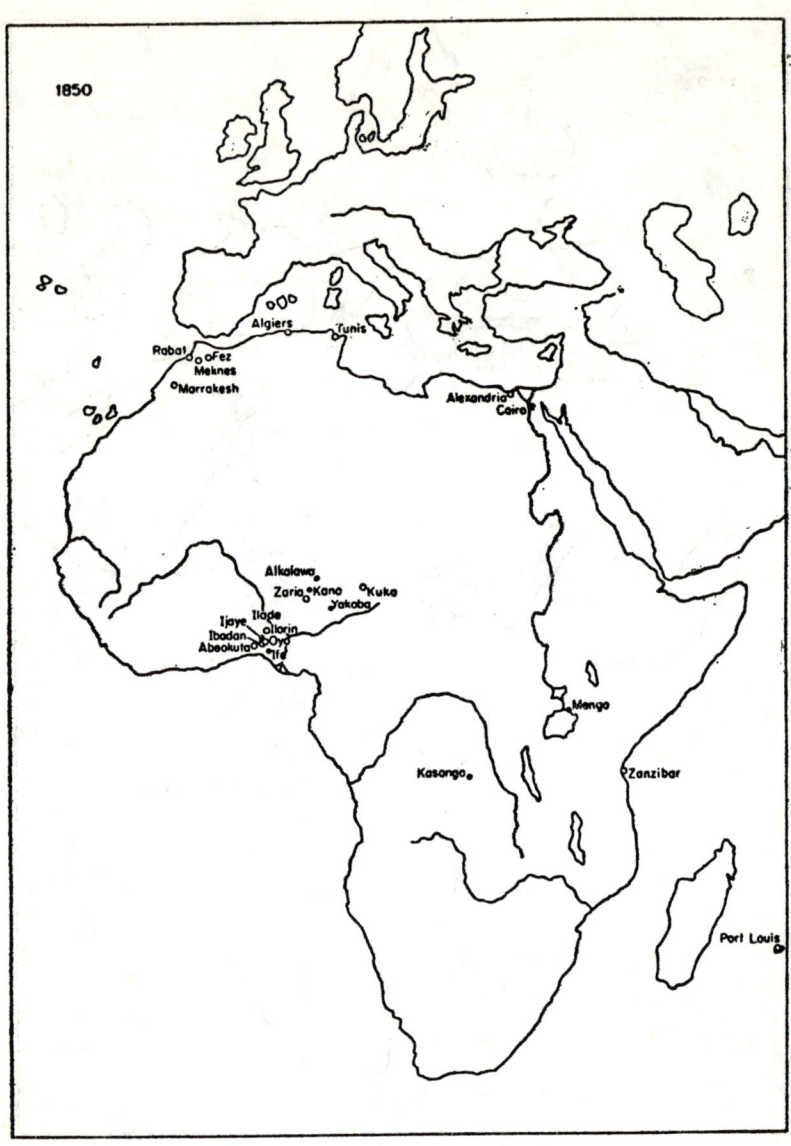

Cities over 20 000 inhabitants in 1850

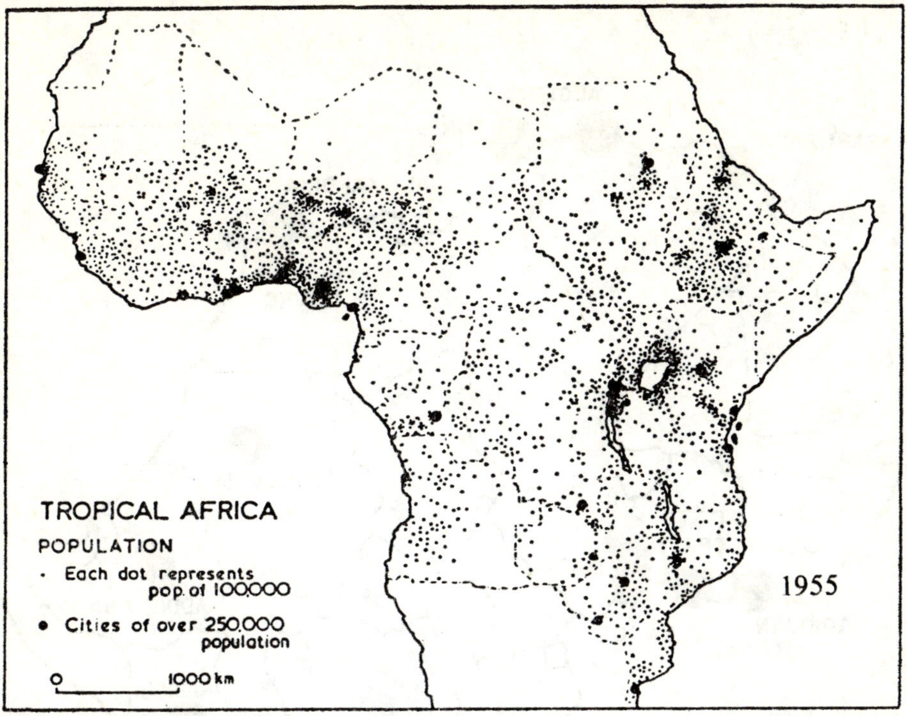

The distribution of population in Tropical Africa based on data available for the late 1960's.

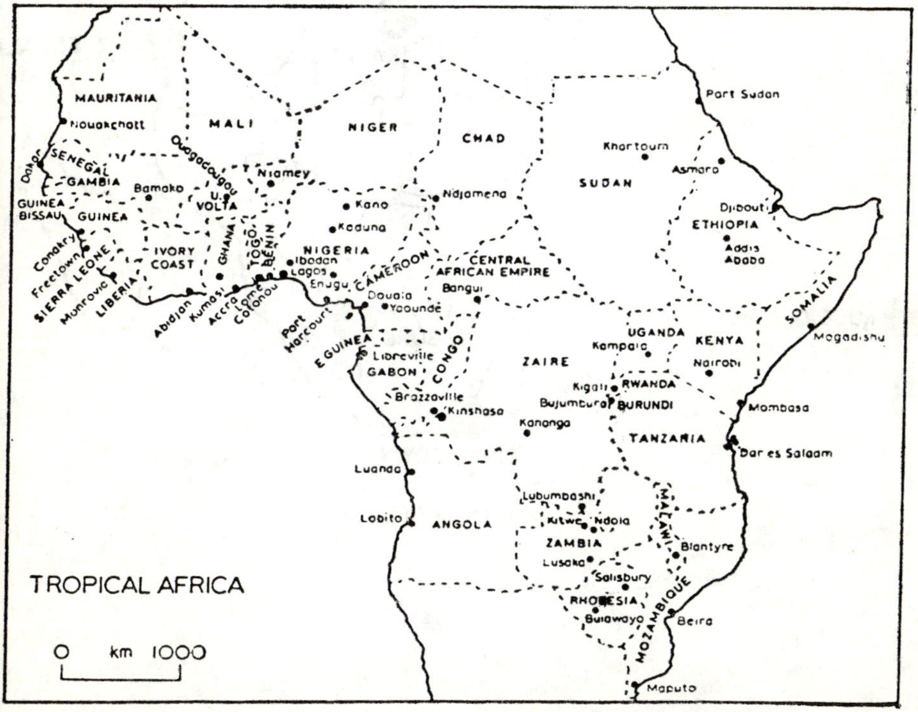

Africa's cities South of Vidal-de-La-Blache's line in the late 1960s

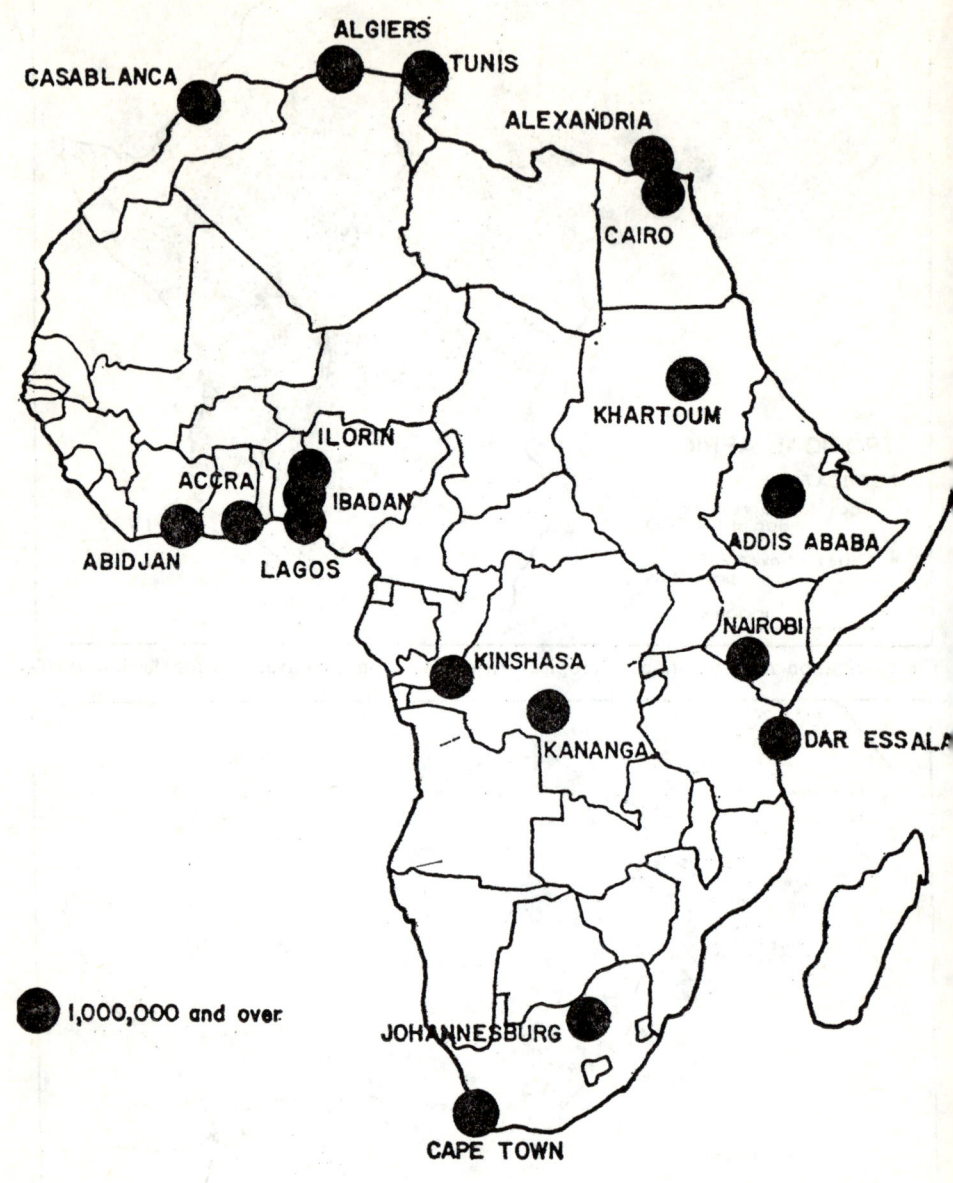

Major cities in Africa (1980)

PREFACE

This work is clearly written in an African perspective. Before undertaking this concise but comprehensive study, we carried out a certain number of expertises – as a sociologist urbanist with experience in Africa, – for academic institutions (Ankerl 1983), and specialized international (regional and world) organizations concerning this subject and in related issues (Ankerl 1980, 1982, 1983a, 1984).

A broad field of study should be limited according to some heuristic principles. In order to be relevant to our mandate, crucial regions, periods and aspects were researched. Since all major countries considered were independent in 1970, – meaning they took legal responsibility for their futures, – we began our study at that point in time, which also allowed an appreciation of the prevailing trends. Why was Tropical Africa – the least urbanized major area of Africa and of the world – chosen?

In all respects Africa itself is part of what Alfred Sauvy coined the *Third World* (Y. Lacoste 14–15). It is a paradoxical grouping, a set of countries with very diverse civilizational backgrounds which have been more (some decades ago) or less (one-and-half centuries ago) recently decolonized. It embraces South America, also one of the most urbanized major areas of the world (Ankerl 1984: 31). The dilemma of the Third World's self-perception lies in the fact that, on the one hand, their common background consists in their dependent colonial past, and on the other hand, the strong reference to this can eclipse their own civilizational pasts – e.g. urbanistic pasts – necessary to cultural self-determination. In contrast to the coherent group of OECD countries, the Third World represents a heterogeneous grouping – like aliens in a country's population – and can be best apprehended as a tricontinental coalition (launched thirty years ago by the Afro-Asiatic Conference in Bandung) for obtaining from OECD and COMECON a better share of power and income in the world's affairs. Africa's settlements' network, itself divided by the Sahara, reflects variously animist, Islamic and different eurocolonial pasts.

The largest part of the Third World is situated in the tropics. Numerous international scientific symposia (*Problèmes de croissance urbaines dans le monde tropique;* Durand-Lasserve; Vennetier; Ankerl 1983) as well as the

Lagos Plan (p. 96, point e) recognize that urbanism and architecture in these regions should meet the requirements of the tropical way of life. Consequently, like European agricultural research results, European "urban problem-solving" cannot simply be transferred to the tropics.

Within Tropical Africa we considered chiefly the largest countries of Eastern, Middle and Western Africa. In reality, urbanizatione (.g. primate city) and economic development (e.g. share of export market) follow different processes according to the size of the country.

In this study we consider the urbanization process in its socioeconomic effects and in relation to social policy. We have already mentioned that Tropical Africa as a whole has the lowest urbanization indicator (i.e., urban population as a percentage of the total population) and the most rapid increase of this indicator among the world's major areas, while South America's urbanization indicator is at the same level as the OECD countries'. However, the significance of this data appears only if we relate it to indicators of socioeconomic development. For practical purposes, we devised an *overurbanization index* and an *urbanization overspeed index* by dividing in the first case the urbanization indicators and in the second case their growth rate (expected and actual points of increase during 1970–2000) by the per capita GDP. The term "overurbanization" has been introduced, among others, by Hoselitz and Davis and Golden. Based on the World Urban Resources Index of Columbia University, they compared past and present cross sections and time series to learn how the urbanization indicator is related to industrialization (Davis and Golden: 15 and 20–23) – resp. to non-agricultural employment – and to identify deviant relationships (they refer to Robert Parke Jr.'s paper about "overurbanization in Egypt" of 1954; cf. Konrád and Szelényi's "underurbanization in socialist countries"). While urbanization and industrialization are not unrelated, we agree with Sovani (120–2) that strictly speaking a prescriptive positive relationship in precise quantitative terms cannot be established between urbanization and industrial employment. We do not use the term "overurbanization" in this sense. Our viewpoint is nearer to Gugler's (1982: 183), Gilbert's (p. (163) and to Friedmann's "hyperurbanization". As a matter of fact, for us urbanization considered as a structural change results mainly from massive rural-urban migration involving not only active populations but sets of whole households (Ankerl 1982). Abandoning a rural habitat and claiming a new one in urban areas burdens the national economy with considerable additional costs (Linn; W. A. Lewis 1978: 39–40; B. W. G. Roberts: 26–44). In terms of the percentage of the GDP, low-income countries have more difficulties in meeting these expenses. To show the relative heaviness of this burden we calculated our overurbanization index and urbanization overspeed index for the world's major areas and for all the 37 low- and middle-income countries which have (1980) at least 10 million inhabitants (fig. 7). While Latin America and even North Africa have higher urbanization indicators than Tropical Africa, it is Tropical Africa which as a whole has not only the highest urbanization overspeed index but also the highest overurbanization index. These indexes are the quotient of a percentage value (multiplied by ten for convenience) and a monetary dimension. Above a certain level of development (Ankerl 1982: 532–33; 1984: 38), the overurbanization and urbanization overspeed indexes lose their significance as they approximate zero, thus vanishing by themselves.

The Table of Contents shows very clearly how we develop our subject, which we consider from the point of view of the *underprivileged*. We tried, however, to avoid common pitfalls of "urban studies": relaxing discipline, handling all socioeconomic problems which occur in cities. Of course, any event happens somewhere – either in urban areas or in the countryside. Here we deal with social problems as far as they are (in our opinion) specifically related to urban places, that is, in contrast to problems concerning the countryside or in relation to it.

This work is an applied study and cannot embrace the whole theory of development. For theoretical underpinning, we referred to three of our previous books where we treat the planning of human investment in economic development (1965, our doctoral work), basic issues of income distribution and redistribution in a market economy (1978) and finally the distinctly spatial aspects of human social behavior (1981). This present succint book does not allow for more development.

Addressed to people deeply interested and involved in the promotion of an autonomous development of Africa, we hope that further studies will contribute to make this field of study more systematically explored than it has been in the past, since we have acquired the conviction that for efficient and rapid relief for the developing countries in their present need, a more *systematic approach sustaining continuity in the effort* is more essential than any foreign financial aid: even the most generous and desinterested.

This volume has profited from the very efficient and dedicated editorial work of Stephanie Shine.

Professor Guy Ankerl

The Graduate Institute of Development Studies
University of Geneva
August 1985

CHAPTER ONE

REVIEW OF BASIC DATA OF URBANIZATION SINCE INDEPENDENCE
(1970—2000)

Problems related to rapid urbanization are visible to the naked eye in large cities in Tropical Africa. However, we cannot assess the situation, point to grave cases and devise solutions without having, on the one hand, basic facts of the principal aspects of the process and their interrelatedness, and on the other hand, a viewpoint which makes explicit what might be considered positive change, i.e., progress.

Data come from census, survey and case studies. Concerning census data, unfortunately it is not within the scope of this study to discuss the reliability of the data published by relevant UN offices — with the exception of obvious errors — nor the method of estimates and projections exposed in *Manual VIII: Methods for Projections of Urban and Rural Population* (UN: E. 1974. XIII. 3).

Furthesmore we must chiefly limit our studies to the 5 largest countries of Tropical Africa which have at least ten million inhabitants: *Nigeria* and *Ghana* in Western Africa, *Zaire* in Middle Africa and *Tnazania* and *Kenya* in Eastern Africa. Data about other countries in Tropical Africa will seldom be represented and will be used to point out the extreme cases. At any rate, for all «problem-sampling» small and large countries must be considered separately (McGranahan: 17). Data from other continents appears for comparison. World averages serve the same purpose.

STATE OF URBANIZATION IN 1980

An *urbanization indicator* is the proportion of population living in urban areas. *Globally* Tropical Africa was one of the *less urbanized areas* of the world in 1980.

Regional variation of the urbanization indicator is considerable within this area: Eastern Africa   16%
  Western Africa   22%
  Middle Africa   34%

A great range of variation also appears when we consider each country. On the low end Burundi has 2.3% as an urbanization indicator and on the top Equatorial Guinea with 54%, both small countries. Among the 5 countries with at least ten million inhabitants Tanzania is on the bottom with 12% and *Zaire* on the top has 40%. This variation conforms to the regional one. Between population density and urbanization there is no correlation.

STATE OF AGGLOMERATIONS IN 1980

Administratively defined (resident) "urban population" (*UN Growth*...: 7–10; *UN Patterns* ...: 9) can be spread over a network of relatively dense settlements as nodes (Ankerl 1974, 1981). Each node — city — can be more or less populous (1) and more or less distant (2) from each other. Theories on optimum city size and optimum spatial distribution are based on this aspect of urbanization (Cotten; J. I. Clarke; Urban Primacy in Tropical Africa in *Croissance*: 447–53; J. J. Sprengler; Africa and the Theory of Optimum City Size, in *Miner*: 55–89).

TABLE 1.

Agglomerations of at least a million inhabitants in Tropical Africa, ranked by size, 1980 (Population in millions)

Rank	Population	% of the urban population living in the mentioned city
1. *Kinshasa*	3.09	28
2. *Lagos*	2.50	17
3. *Accra*	1.41	34
4. *Nairobi*	1.28	58
5. Ilorin/Nigeria	1.16	8
6. Kananga/Zaire	1.10	10
7. *Dar es Salaam*	1.08	51
8. Ado-Ekiti/Nigeria	1.00	7

(Source: *UN Patterns*...: table 48)
* Capital cities are in italic.

Tropical Africa's largest city is *Kinshasa* (table 1). As we will see, there are various methods to represent *urban concentration* such as overall primacy index, two-city index, four-city index and rank-size rule (Vining: 147–95; Clarke in *Croissance:* 450–2). Vining establishes the rank-size rule $r \times P^q = K$ where $q \approx 1$, K=constant for a given group of cities, "r" stands for the rank of a particular city in population and "P" for its size, viz. the size of the "n"th city approximates the "n"th of the size of the largest city (cf. F. Auerbach, Zipf). This formula gives a so-called log-normal city-size distribution.

Cameroon, for example, has a log-normal (linear) distribution (Cotten: 348s; Clarke in *Croissance:* 452), while among the five largest countries, in Zaire, Kinshasa, the primate city predominates. It is also the case for Tanzania. (Kenya is in this respect an intermediate case.)

The *spatial* distribution of the agglomeration is again another question. As a matter of fact, in relation to the national territory's center of gravity Kinshasa, Lagos, Accra as well as Dar es Salaam are eccentrically located — sea or port cities, true bridge-heads between the raw material exporting countries and the "West".

In short, the present level of urbanization in this region shows Zaire as the most urbanized large country and its capital, Kinshasa the largest city. Zaire is also representative of Middle Africa which is relatively highly urbanized in Tropical Africa.

TRENDS OF URBANIZATION BETWEEN 1970—2000

We consider past facts (1970) and projections (until 2000) which show the trend as an inherent kinetic characteristic of the present situation. The urbanization indicator is a percentage-type indicator, therefore its growth can be better measured by subtracting ($\triangle$) the initial (%) figure from the latter figure than by the method of measurement of change by (%) of (%). (This latter method has the tendency in case of distributional or percentage-type indicatosr to overrepresent the change occured in case of low initial %. McGranhan: 13).

Concerning the *regions*, according to the projections until 2000, the most urbanized Middle Africa will increase its urbanization indicator more than the other less urbanized regions of Africa; therefore, the *gulf* between the less urbanized Eastern Africa and Middle Africa (the latter of which will be more than 50% urbanized) will increase. Tropical Africa as a whole will increase its urbanization indicator much more rapidly than the rest of the world, and Middle Africa in particular will reach in 2000 the average urbanization level of the world.

Concerning individual *countries,* some small ones (Malawi, Benin) have the highest increase in their urbanization indicator between 1970 and 2000; however, their cases must be separated from those of larger countries. McGranahan rightly observes:

... small countries have significant and consistant differences from large countries in their development profiles, at whatever level of development and in whatever part of the world. (1979: 17)

TABLE 2.

Growth of urbanization indicator (increase in %)

Region and country	Urbanization indicator		Growth between			
	1970	2000	2000–1970 (2)–(1)	1970–1980	1980–1990	1990–2000
	(1)	(2)	(3)	(4)	(5)	(6)
By region						
Eastern Africa (E)	10.7	29.4	18.7	5.45	6.58	6.69
Western Africa (W)	17.2	35.9	18.7	5.02	6.36	7.27
Middle Africa (M)	25.2	51.6	36.4	9.21	9.28	7.91
By country				Populations density. Persons per km^2		
					1970	1979
Malawi (E)	9.3	68.0	58.7			
Benin (W)	16.0	54.4	38.4			
1. Zaire (M)	30.3	56.3	26		9	12
2. Ghana (W)	29.1	51.2	22.1		36	47
3. Tanzania (E)	6.9	25.0	18.1		14	18
4. Nigeria (W)	16.4	33.4	17		61	81
5. Kenya (E)	10.2	26.2	16		19	26

Among the 5 largest countries, *Zaire* already has the highest urbanization indicator and increases this indicator at the *fastest pace;* therefore, *differentiation* between urbanized and rural countries in Africa will increase. This statement should be qualified. In fact, the detailed analysis of the three decades between 1970 and 2000 shows that while Zaire does not accelerate its urbanization, the other 4 countries do. On the other hand, table 2 shows that there is no positive correlation between the urbanization process and population density. While Zaire has the highest increase in its urbanization indicator, it has the lowest growth rate of population among the 5 largest countries, and Kenya, which has the highest growth rate of population, has the smallest increase of its urbanization indicator (16%). We again see to which degree *Zaire* is more specifically characterized by its *rapid urbanization* (very rapid in respect to worldwide context as well) than by its rapid population growth. (Population data from *World Development Report:* 166.)

TRENDS IN URBAN CONCENTRATION AND IN THE DEVELOPMENT OF AGGLOMERATIONS BETWEEN 1970—2000

In order to assess trends of agglomerations, we can either compare their development (e.g. primate city versus the second largest city in a country) or the primate city's development with the country's urbanization process. In the latter case we consider urban concentration and the relevant comparison is between the rate of the primate city's population and the country's urban population. (Thus the overall population growth can be disregarded and the *net* urban concentration calculated for which the urbanization indicator is not directly relevant.)

We can consider the 8 cities which have at least one million inhabitants (table 1) or extend the list to all 33 which will have that in 2000 (table 4). Since we consider the urban population growth only in terms of the 5 largest countries of Tropical Africa (table 3), for the urban concentration only the metropoles situated there can be studied.

TABLE 3.

Growth of urban population in the 5 largest countries

Country and region	Urban population in millions		Growth rate in %
	1970 (1)	2000 (2)	(3) = ×100(2)/(1)
1. Tanzania	0.92	8.51	925
2. Kenya	1.15	8.13	707
3. Nigeria	9.01	45.0	500
4. Ghana	2.51	10.8	430
5. Zaire	6.56	27.8	424
Total	20.15	100.24	497
Less developed region	651	2116	325
World total	1354	3208	237

The growth rate of the 33 cities which will probably have over one million inhabitants in 2000 (table 4) varies between 1239% (Dar es Salaam) and 239% (Ibadan). (The capital of Senegal, Dakar, will also have only a growth rate of 323%) All these largest 33 cities of Tropical Africa have a growth rate higher than that of the world urban population in general, and than that of the urban population of the less developed countries on the average (tables 3 and 4).

The growth rate of the 8 cities which already have one million inhabitants (tables 1 and 4), ranges between 1239% (Dar es Salaam) and 500% (Lagos). *Dar es Salaam* has the highest growth rate but all 8 cities will have very high growth rates.

The breaking down of the trends between 1970 and 2000 into decennial components shows that the growth is continuous but the pace of increase slows down, with a few exceptions (table 4).

TABLE 4.

Growth rate of large cities in Tropical Africa between 1970–2000, cities which have more than a million inhabitants in 2000
(Population in millions)

City	Country	Population		Increase in percentage			
		1970	2000	1970–2000	1970–1980	1980–1990	1990–2000
		(1)	(2)	(3)	(4)	(5)	(6)
DAR ES SALAAM	Tanz.	0.375	4.65	1239	287	231	187
Kikwit	Zaïre	0.121	1.44	1188	326	224	162
ILORIN	Niger.	0.396	4.52	1140	295	217	178
Cotonou	Benin	0.204	2.31	1130	336	225	153
ADO-EKITI	Niger.	0.346	3.45	996	290	195	176
Mushin	Niger.	0.259	2.57	992	269	208	178
Ila	Niger.	0.200	1.95	976	266	206	178
NAIROBI	Kenya	0.550	4.87	885	231	209	185
Kampala	Ugand.	0.357	3.02	845	228	205	181
Lusaka	Zamb.	0.299	2.51	840	265	193	164
Blantyre-Limbe	Malawi	0.148	1.20	811	238	222	153
KANANGA	Zaïre	0.449	3.28	731	247	191	158
Maputo	Mozam.	0.375	2.62	698	200	190	182
Conakry	Guinea	0.330	2.30	677	231	183	166
Luanda	Angola	0.465	2.90	630	206	183	167
KINSHASA	Zaïre	1.370	8.41	615	225	180	151
Douala	Camer.	0.250	1.45	596	210	187	151
Zaria	Niger.	0.229	1.34	586	194	174	173
Mogadiscio	Somal.	0.190	1.10	579	198	180	161
Freetown	Sier. L.	0.202	1.11	547	192	173	160
Kitwe	Zamb.	0.115	1.20	540	200	116	161
Ede	Niger	0,187	1.04	540	190	173	174
Kaduna	Niger.	0.239	1.91	522	235	179	176
Bamako	Mali	0.249	1.29	518	177	174	169
ACCRA	Ghana	0.754	3.84	510	188	174	176
Abidjan	Ivor. C.	0.356	1.80	506	192	174	160
LAGOS	Niger.	1.390	6.95	500	181	165	167
Mombasa	Kenya	0.256	1.19	466	154	166	181
Ogbomosho	Niger.	0.177	1.73	423	160	156	169
Kumasi	Ghana	0.350	1.40	403	161	161	156
Kano	Niger.	0.335	1.28	381	150	154	169
Dakar	Seneg.	0.559	1.88	323	145	149	154
Ibadan	Niger.	0.725	1.73	239	134	134	134

Note: Cities listed in capital letters have already at least one million inhabitants. Capital cities are in italic.
Source: *UN Patterns*... 1980.

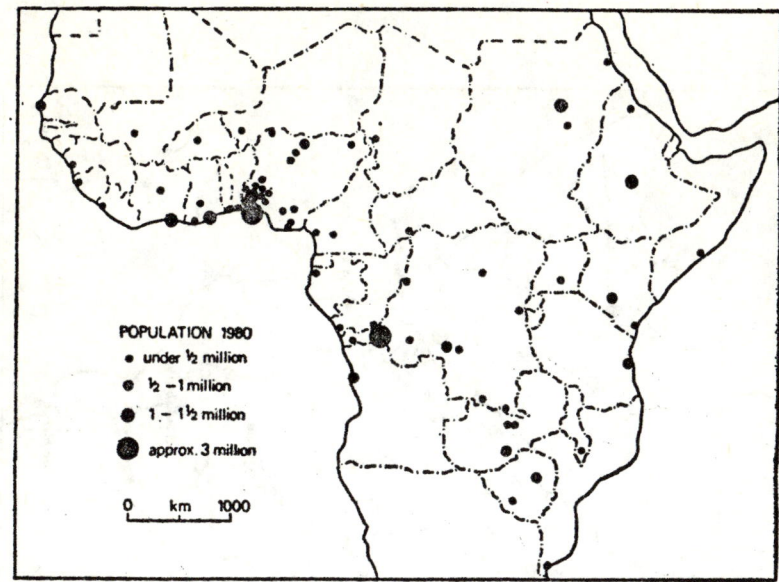

Tropical Africa: distribution of cities in 1980

As we can expect for statistical reasons, the 8 presently largest cities are all situated in the 5 largest countries of the region and growth of these 8 cities reflects the growth of these countries' urban population.

More specifically we pose the question: is the general urbanization process in these countries outpaced by the rapidity of urban concentration? As we mentioned in the section *"State of Urbanization"*, urban concentration can be measured by more or less sophisticated indexes. The index can be constructed by dividing the primate city's populaton either by the country's whole urban population, or by the second largest city's population (two-city index), or by the total population of the next three largest cities (fow-city index; Jeffersen; Zipf; Clarke in *Croissance:* 449–52; Subramanian and others in the periodical *Economic Development and Cultural Change*).

Considering urban concentration growth by the overall primacy city index (table 5), in all 5 countries except Nigeria, the urban concentration outpaces the growth of the country's urban population in general. Among the 5 large countries, it is again Zaire which occupies the first rank. Zaire with the lowest population growth has the highest urbanization indicator presently and the most rapid growth of this indicator. Yet, according to the urban concentration index used in table 5 it is Zaire where the urban concentration process is the most pronounced in respect to its capital,

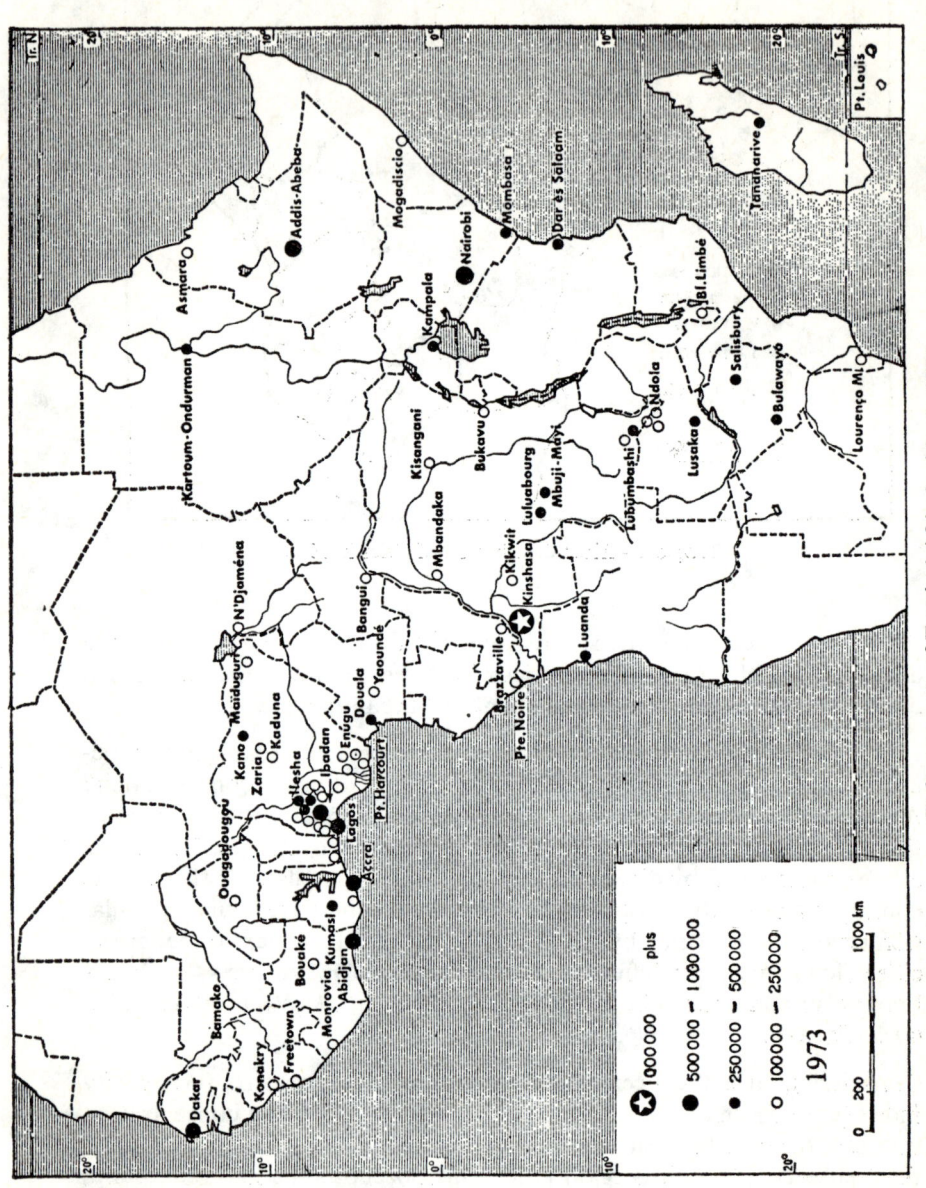

Reference map of Tropical Africa's cities in 1973

TABLE 5.

Growth rate of the urban population and the primate city between 1970 and 2000

	Growth rate		Growth of urban concentration (3)=(1)/(2)
	of primate city (%)	of urban population (%)	
	(1)	(2)	(3)
1. Kinshasa/Zaire	615	425	1.45
2. Dar es Salaam/Tanzania	1239	924	1.34
3. Nairobi/Kenya	885	710	1.25
4. Accra/Ghana	510	432	1.18
5. Lagos/Nigeria	500	600	0.83

Kinshasa. For this very reason Kinshasa is and remains the largest city of Tropical Africa in this century, despite the fact that Zaisre' two-city index decreases (table 6) and that Zaire has less than half of Nigeria's population. The two-city index shows that *Kananga*'s congestion will be even worse than Kinshasa's. However, Zaire's city-size distribution curve remains the so-called primate type (Clarke in *Croissance:* 452).

Dar es Salaam has the highest growth rate among the metropoles. In reality, Tanzania's urbanization process (table 2) can be considered more an urban concentration phenomenon than one of urbanization in general. *Kenya*'s relatively slow urbanization process (table 2) is accompanied by the highest population growth rate (*World Development...:* 166) and, on the other hand, by a tendency to strong urban concentration (table 6). The growth of its two-city index anticipates that Kenya's rank-size distribution

TABLE 6.

Two-city index

Country	City	Year 1970	Year 2000
Zaire	Kinshasa/Kananga	3.30	2.56
Kenya	Nairobi/Mombasa	2.15	4.09
Ghana	Accra/Kumasi	2.15	2.74
Nigeria	Lagos/Ibadan Ilorin	1.90	2.00

Note: Nigeria's two-city index involves different cities in 1970 and 2000, we also calculated its four-city index Lagos/(Ilorin+Ado-Ekiti+Mushin): 1.39 (1970) and 0.66 (2000).

curve will possibly change from its present convex (or intermediate) shape to the primate-city curve.

Ghana's urbanization shows an intermediate situation (table 2) with a slight tendency to urban concentration (tables 5 and 6); however, Ghana's rank-size distribution curve will probably preserve its near log-normal shape.

Nigeria has among the 5 large countries a relatively slow urbanization process (table 2) and the preeminence of its primate city, Lagos, will even fade somewhat (tables 5 and 6; cf Amin: 9–20 and L. Green in Amin). Its four-city index is even lower than Cameroon's (Cotten; Clarke in *Croissance;* Fapohunda: 33): both countries have a federal political structure. The diminishing of Nigeria's four-city index from 1.39 to 0.66 (table 6) anticipates that this country preserves its near log-normal rank-size distribution curve. Therefore, Nigeria's urbanization probably brings more drsatic changes to Ilorin, Ado-Ekiti, Mushin, Ila as well as to Abuja, the Federal Capital Territory than to Lagos (table 4). *(UN Patterns... 1980)*.

ACTIVITIES AND URBANIZATION

Until now we described the phenomenon of urbanization passively as a change in residential statistics. In order to present data independently from the actors' intents, we did not consider the inhabitant as an active human being. However, if the authority is to influence the urbanization process, it should consider the inhabitant as an autonomous beingw ho is active and whose activities are meaningful. Concerning the urbanization process, which activities should be considered principally?

In general terms, man looks for a framework where he can realize his aspirations in accordance with his life-cycle (Ankerl 1965). He should have at his disposal the means in general and the habitat in particular.

– Man is not a snail — he is neither born with nor migrates with his shell (even if nomads try to adapt this strategy to their life-style by transportable tents). Increase in urban population dictates the need for new urban habitat. To assess the task, above all, data must be known about slums and shantytowns, optimistically called spontaneous settlements.

– In order to solve problems, sufficient productive means should be at society's disposal. With the increase in the number of inhabitants, usually more working hands are also available to be organized efficiently to respond to the challenge, of cosure, if the productive forces are developed and maintained with foreisght: manpower formed, equipped with tools, and supplied with natural resources. For this very reason urbanization data should be studied in relation to some basic economic data.

– Urbanization itself results from human activities described by demography, either from migration or from so-called natural increase, i.e. birth-death balances in rural and urban areas. If by policy design the authority is to change the trend of the urbanization process, the source of the process should be known. In a second step, if it is known that migration is the main source, sample survey and case study must show whether the differences of means of subsistence, i.e. job opportunities, lead to rural-urban migration. The cost-benefit analysis will give important indications as to whichs olution is preferable in a country's specific historical context; either the population should migrate to urban areas or the investment should be increased in rural areas (mobility of population versus mobility of capital).

1. Demographic sources of urban growth

Due to the fact that many decision-makers share the anti-urban bias of a large part of the population, appraisals of urban growth are often incorrect and thus remedies for unwanted development are inappropriate. We often hear, for example, that since the natural population increase is "obviously" higher in the "healthier" rural areas than in the urban areas, the urban growth comes from migration. We now take an analytical look at this matter.

Indeed, we should distinguish (a) growth rate of the urban population and (b) the growth rate of the urbanization indicator. The first represents the gross population growht in urban areas, while the second shows urbanization as a structural change.

With regard to the source of urban growth, we can distinguish (1) the natural increase of the population in general, (2) the difference in the natural increase of the population in rural and urban areas, and (3) the net rural-urban migration.

Growth of the urban population comes from (1), (2) and (3), while that of the urbanization indicator only from (2) and (3). Let us now consider these sources individually.

Migration includes in the census reclassification which is either (a) a boundary expansion of urban areas or (b) a graduation of previously rural areas into the status of urban ones (or vice versa), or even a redefinition of rural settlements. Authors (V. I. Perevedentsev, Eui-Young Yu) usually estimate that ca 25% of this source is attributable to reclassification.

Natural increase results from birth rate and age-specific survival (or death) rate. For developing countries, this latter rate is higher in urban areas than in rural ones. Because these countries have mostly youthful populations, this difference does not play a significant role statistically, but means that rural areas are not necessarily healthier than urban ones. The overall natural increase is somewhat better in rural than in urban areas, but in developed countries the difference is bigger (1:1.07) than in developing ones (1:1.06).

Urban population increase in the developing countries is attributable mainly to internal migrations and reclassification, but in developing countries it is chiefly due to natural increase of the urban population. (For 40 countries considered between 1960 and 1970 the contribution of the natural increase is 61%. In this sample Tropical Africa is represented only by Ghana. *UN Patterns...*: table 11.) If we add to this picture that approximately 25% of the "migration and reclassification" is attributable to reclassification, the urban population growth generated from geographic mobility is only about 30% in the less developed world. In relation to Tropical Africa, this statement must be qualified in two respects: these data neglect international migration which is in some areas unchecked and high, and, on the other hand, where the urban growth is very rapid, the migration's contribution in terms of percentage is somewhat higher (*UN Patterns...*: 25, 27).

The conclusion is that even if the government prevents migration into urban areas, only "one third" of the problem is solved.

In regard to the *structural change* represented by the growth of the urbanization indicator, viz. the relative growth of the urban population, it is the in-migration and reclassification which are the principal sources of the increase.

If we try to assess the situation specifically for Tropical Africa in quantitative terms, we again lack reliable and comparable data.

Tanzania, for example, changed its definition of rural and urban areas which makes any intercensal rate calculation between 1960 and 1970 impossible (*UN Patterns...*: 22). We have some data from Ita I. Ekanem's case study (*UN Patterns...*: 23 n. 8) about medium sized towns in Nigeria. We have the required data only from Ghana.

Natural increase causes 58% of Ghana's urban population growth. And if we deduct the reclassification (1/4 of the migration data), the natural increase contributes about 75% of the urban population increase. In contrast, growth of Ghana's urbanization indicator is mainly attributable to migration (84%), and higher natural increase in urban areas compared to rural ones is far behind in second place (16%). (Our calculation is based on table 15 of *UN Patterns* and on the hypothesis concerning reclassification. We neglected international migration which can affect the result if it is quantitatively different in rural and urban areas.)

By way of general conclusion, the first task for Tropical Africa is to collect systematically at least basic data in order to constitute time series and interregional comparisons.

2. Production and urbanization

Important literature is available about the occupational characteristics of the population and its location in rural and urban areas. As we discussed elsewhere (Ankerl 1965: 78, 96), some doctrines posit that a society's economic efficiency develops with the increase of the proportion of the labor forces engaged in the non-agrarian sector—a sign of structural transformation. For the developed countries, this doctrine has been refined by the post-industrial concept (B.D. Bell), meaning the stabilization of the proportion employed in the industrial sector and the growth of the proportion of active population engaged in the tertiary or service sector (Colin Clark, Fourastié). By taking into account the recent proliferation of the informal service sector in the less developed countries, the growth of the proportion of the population occupied in industry has been considered for these regions as the essential sign of economic progress ("agrarian" versus "industrial population"). Some authors accept this thesis and have supplemented it with another specifying a desired relationship between industrialization and urbanization. Among others, Hoselitz states that compared to earlier historical examples, present developing countries are overurbanized, namely the percentage of the labor force in industry divided by the percentage of the population living in urban areas is too low; this is an anomaly which hinders the development of the economic efficiency of these societies. In this line of thought, without an indication of any optimal ratio, a maximalization should be considered as a desirable policy objective. This policy is largely pursued in the collectivistic countries (Gur Ofer: 219-44).

In fact, the above mentioned ratio was very stable world-wide around 1:2 and its rate of growth between 1950 and 1970 varied in the world between 1.21 (for USSR) and 0.722 (for Western South Asia). During the same period Eastern Africa presents a regression of 0.888 and Middle Africa a regression of 0.941, while Western Africa progressed somewhat by 1.09 (ILO 1977; *UN Patterns...*: table 9). In this respect we note that Cole (p. 123, table 4.1) established a strong positive correlation (+0.92) between the non-agricultural population and the urbanization indicator in international comparison based on data from 60 countries including the 5 largest countries of Tropical Africa.

In order to assess the effect of these structural indicators upon the economic development, they must be contrasted with some measure of the development of the overall economic performance of the country. A usual measure of the economic development is the *GNP, GDP* or *NMP* per capita.[1] Considering either (a) the growth rate of the proportion of the labor force in industry or (b) the growth rate of the ratio of industrial population to urban population, neither one shows a strictly positive correlation with an economic development indicator.

Even if strict imitation of Europe's XIXth century were the prescription for the developing countries, Hoselitz's doctrine would remain open to question (Sjoberg: 5; Reiman: 2–3; Beling and Totten; see also *UN Patterns*...: table 3).

In respect to the relation between economic indicators and urbanization, our concern here is another one: structural change whatsoever in a society compared to a stationary situation — causes the country additional charges requiring supplementary resources. On the other hand, we posit that countries with higher per capita income are more able to bear the increased charges and cope with the emerging problems (housing, increased load on public services: transport, communication, water, sewage, etc. Gugler 1982). An indicator such as *GDP* per capita which reflects the overall state of the economic development also has the advantage (over structural indicators such as industrialization indicators) of reflecting this development without privileging one or another mode of development. We should aslo bear in mind that the *GDP* and other indicators which are based on the National Accounts are not without distortion; namely the output of all economic activities outside the accounted (monetary and taxable) market trade such as self-consumption in households and agrarian subsistence economy, production in the informal or quarternary (Y. Friedman) or do-it-yourself activities which are important especially in less developed countries are insufficiently taken into account (Seer: 193–209; Morris: 7–8).

In table 7, we present a comprehensive survey of the world's largest countries (viz. having at least ten million inhabitants) in the low-income (li) and middle-income (mi) groups (incomes measured by their *GNP* per capita), concerning their urbanization indicators (1980) and especially the expected growth of these indicators between 1970 and 2000 in relation to their *GNP* per capita and *GDP* per capita in 1979 (or 1978). In table 7, column 4 proposes to show roughly how a country's urbanization is related to its level of economic development *(overurbanization index)* and the indexes in columns 5 and 6 show how each country's economic means fail to keep level with the burden caused by the increase in urbanization *(urbanization overspeed index)*. If we take stock of the 13 countries in the li-group and the 24 in the mi-group, we can make the following statements:

– The urbanization indicators of the mi-group range higher than those of the li-group, nevertheless, the increases in the urbanization indicators range higher in the mi-group than in the li-group. This means that the existing difference in urbanization between mi- and li-group countries does not diminish.

– The problem appears when we compare the urbanization with the economic development. Cole (121, table 4.10) found a positive correlation (+0.76) between the urbanization indicator and the country's *GNP* per capita. In reality it seems that the urbanization takes off earlier than the economic development. The index in column 4 of table 7 shows that the low-income countries are more urbanized in relation to their "developmental level" (expressed in *GNP* per capita) than the middle-income countries.

– The rate of the li-group countries' urbanization growth compared to the mi-group countries' growth advances even more clearly. Indeed, in column 5 of table 7, we find practically all li-group countries have higher indexes than any mi-group country. If we now make the same comparison in terms of *GDP* per capita instead of *GNP* per capita, all li-group countries (without exception) have a higher urbanization overspeed index (column 6) than any mi-group country.

In this respect, it should be noted that our overurbanization index and urbanization overspeed index are quotients between a percentage and a monetary magnitude, and above a certain level of economic development they vanish by approximate zero.

What conclusion can we draw for our proper subject of study: where among the 5 largest countries of Tropical Africa is the urbanization growth for economic reasons overpaced?

Among these 5 countries the two countries — Zaire and Tanzania — which are in the li-group have the highest urbanization overspeed index. Calculated in terms of *GDP* per capita (column 1b of Table 7), the urbanization overspeed index has a monotonic progression, inverse to the progression of *GDP* per capita (column 6). The same monotonic relation exists in respect to the overurbanization index (column 4 of table 7). In short, the basic problem is that the rapid urbanization process in Tropical Africa is not matched by the region' seconomic growth.

TABLE 7.

"Overurbanization" index and "urbanization overspeed" index of low- and middle-income countries, 1970–2000

Major area, region and country	GNP per capita 1979 (or 1978)	GDP per capita 1979 (or 1978*)	Urban-ization indi-cator 1980	Growth in (2) 1970–2000	$\frac{(2)}{(1a)} \times 10$	$\frac{(3)}{(1a)} \times 10$	$\frac{(3)}{(1b)} \times 10$
	(1a)	(1b)	(2)	(3)	(4)	(5)	(6)
World	2110	–	39.3	14.0	0.19	0.066	–
Africa	250	–	28.9	19.6	1.16	0.78	–
South Asia	280	–	24.0	15.6	0.86	0.56	–
Latin America	1350	–	64.7	17.8	0.48	0.13	–
USSR	3700	–	64.8	19.4	0.18	0.05	–
Europe	5680	–	68.8	13.2	0.12	0.02	–
North America	9660	–	73.7	10.3	0.08	0.01	–
Bangladesh	90	118	11.2	14.6	1.24	1.62	1.24
Ethiopia	130	143	14.5	19.0	1.12	1.46	1.33
Nepal	140	119	5.0	5.8	0.36	0.42	0.49
Burma	140	133	27.1	18.0	1.94	1.29	1.35
Afghanistan	170	241	15.4	17.0	0.91	1.00	0.71
Vietnam	130	–	22.8	18.1	1.75	1.39	–
India	190	184*	22.3	14.4	1.17	0.76	0.78
Sri Lanka	230	183	24.0	18.7	1.04	0.81	1.02
China	320	–	20.0	15.0	0.63	0.47	–
Pakistan	260	257*	28.2	16.2	1.08	0.62	0.63
Tanzania	260	260*	11.8	18.1	0.45	0.70	0.70
Zaire	260	220	39.5	26.0	1.52	1.00	1.18
Indonesia	340	340*	20.2	15.2	0.59	0.45	0.45
Kenya	380	370*	14.2	16.0	0.37	0.42	0.43
Ghana	400	900	35.9	22.1	0.90	0.55	0.25
Egypt	480	560	45.4	15.1	0.95	0.31	0.27
Thailand	590	480	14.4	10.0	0.24	0.17	0.21
Philippines	600	510	36.2	17.9	0.60	0.30	0.35
Nigeria	670	730	20.4	17.0	0.30	0.17	0.23
Peru	730	670	67.4	21.6	0.92	0.30	0.32
Morocco	447	650	40.6	20.3	0.91	0.45	0.31
Colombia	1010	890	70.2	21.2	0.70	0.21	0.24
Korea (North)	1130	–	59.7	22.9	0.53	0.20	–
Turkey	1330	1160	47.3	25.0	0.36	0.19	0.22
Malaisia	1370	1190	29.4	14.6	0.21	0.11	0.12
Korea (South)	1480	–	54.8	30.7	0.37	0.21	–
Algeria	1590	1250	60.9	30.8	0.38	0.19	0.25
Mexico	1640	1410	66.7	18.4	0.41	0.11	0.13
Chile	1690	1290	81.1	12.4	0.48	0.07	0.10
South Africa	1720	1590	49.6	12.5	0.29	0.07	0.08
Brazil	1780	1640	65.0	20.8	0.37	0.12	0.13
Romania	1900	–	47.9	23.2	0.25	0.12	–
Iran	–	2340	–	–	–	–	–
Argentina	2230	2590	82.4	10.0	0.37	0.04	0.04
Yugoslavia	2430	–	42.3	19.1	0.17	0.08	–
Venezuela	3120	3020	83.3	13.5	0.27	0.04	0.04
Spain	4380	4000	74.3	20.0	0.17	0.05	0.05

Individually, it is again *Zaire* which is in the most critical situation. If we correct the *GNP* by *GDP* per capita, Zaire is the poorest country among the 5 largest countries. Among the large low-income countries, in the whole world only Burma (1.35), Ethiopia (1.33) and Bangladesh (1.24) face a graver problem of urbanization overspeed (column 6 of table 7) but all these are presently less overurbanized than Zaire (column 4). Zaire's overurbanization index is 1.52 and its urbanization overspeed index is 1.18. (Among the smaller countries of Tropical Africa, Malawi has both a higher overurbanization index (1.92) as well as a higher urbanization overspeed index (3.35) than Zaire).

3. Housing and urbanization: proportion of slums and shantytowns in urban areas

> Our ambition as you know, is the elimination of all slums in the Ivory Coast within the next decade. (September 25, 1965. President F. Houphouet-Boigny)
> Everything leads one to belive that these increasing and more rational efforts will entirely fulfill the commitment of 1975 when "There will be no more slums in the Ivory Coast". (Town Planning, Ministry of Informatin. Abidjan, 1968)

Convenient housing depends either on (1) the household's capacity to construct its own home (capacity in terms of land use, tools, materials and know-how) or on (2a) income to rent or buy a house or an apartment and on (2b) the ability to find the desired habitation on the market (Ankerl 1978). In urban settlement the second way is the usual one. Here we will not try to explain the reasons of inadequate housing but we will examine the extent of the problem. How many people live in slums and shantytowns? There is a physical difference between lsums and shantytowns. A slum is a highly congested residential area characterized by deteriorated unsanitary buildings, while as hantytown is a section of a city or town where the houses are small crude buildings or small poorly built huts, huts usually made of wood for temporary use. Both have in common, first of all, health hazards, and in broader terms, they do not allow the inhabitants, or some category of inhabitants, e.g., children to fulfill their perceived legitimate goals (cf. Ankerl 1983).

Before interpretation of the data in table 8, we should consider the quality of the data. Most of the data comes from the *UN Wold Housing Survey* (E/C. 6/129, Geneva, Sept. 5, 1973) and the UN Economic Comission for Africa (1976: 78). In order to construct time series, these data are completed from UNCHBP: *The Improvement of Slums and Squatters Settlements* (New York, 1971: 21–3), from UN Documentation of the Conference in Vancouver (A./Conf. 70/A/1, New York, 1976) and from Granotier (94–5). If we contrast all these data, we find very significant discrepancies. The *UN World Housiug Survey* estimates for example, that 48% of Lusaka's population lives in slums and uncontrolled settlements, while Granotier estimates it at 27% for the same year (1967). The weak data basis for Africa is again an impediment for scientific analysis.

TABLE 8.

Percentage of city population living in slums (and uncontrolled settlements)

City	Year	%	Year	%	Number of inhabitants in 1970 (thousands)	Population growth between 1960 and 1970
Yaoundé	1970	90			178	(198)
Douala	1970	80			250	144
Ibadan	1971	75			725	125
Lomé	1970	75			150	(182)
Mombasa	1970	66			256	158
Kinshasa	1969	60	1964	40	1370	269
Abidjan	1964	60			1190	180
Dakar	1971	60	1969	30	559	150
Accra	1968	53			754	190
Ouagadougou	1966	52			100	160
Blantyre	1966	56			148	(150)
Dar es Salaam	1970	50	1967	34	375	229
Monrovia	1970	50			–	–
Nairobi	1970	48			550	238
Lusaka	1967	48	1967	27	299	(265)

Data in refers to the period between 1970–1980.

On the other hand, some data discrepancy in various publications also comes from differences in definition. Too many people from Nordic countries define substandard housing for frost-free or tropical climates in tneir own way (Ankerl 1983). UN Economic Comission for Africa (1976: 15) rightly states

> ... in certain cultures combined with climate conditions a large number of persons per room seems quite acceptable, because the dwelling is often used only at night by all the household members.

The need for an ecological "relativization" of the habitat becomes clear even within the borders of a isngle continent. Indeed, people's interest in better housing is notably different in Saxon and Latin (or Mediterranean) Europe (e.g. Stockholm versus Paris).

The most appropriate basis for policy use is the comparison between housing in rural and urban areas in the *same* country. It should not be forgotten, however, that rural and urban habitat have specific contexts. If we now compare the data at our disposal, according to experts, in cities of Tropical Africa 10% to 52% of the population is housed decently. In Latin America the situation is similar but in Asia it seems to be somewhat better (Granotier: 95).

In table 8, we considered 15 cities' slum population (1) in relation to the city's size (2) and growth rate (3) in Tropical Africa. The result is that on the one hand, we do not have enough reliable data to establish time series and, on the other hand, inter-city comparisons do not indicate any correlation between development of slums and city size or growth of the cities. However, we can conclude again that among the largest cities of the 5 largest countries of Tropical Africa (Lagos is not listed), Zaire's capital, Kinshasa has the highest percentage of people living in slums and shantytowns. This is even more dramatic if we consider that Zaire has among these 5 largest countries the lowest *GDP* per capita (table 7 column 1b).

NOTES

1. *World Development Report:* 17, 132, 134–5; *1980 World Bank Atlas*. Besides the well-known *GNP*, the *NMP*, meaning Net Material Product, is used in the System of Material Product Balances (MPS) of the National Accounts of the centrally planned economies. Gross Domestic Product is a refinement of the *GNP* for international comparison. Indeed, the *ICP* (International Comparison Profile) compares price ratios for 153 expenditure categories within the total *GDP*. This weighted calculation of purchasing-power exchange rate instead of simple exchange rate makes the comparison more realistic because it also includes articles which do not enter international trade and disregards the fluctuation of the exchange rate, which is nowadays often as high as 20%. This mode of calculation increases income estimates for some low-income countries, especially oil exporters, substantially. Unfortunately, while the UN World Statistics indicate *GDP* per capita, World Bank continues to rank countries according to their *GNP* per capita.
(*GDP:* total yearly flow of goods and services produced by the economy. *GNP: GDP* plus the income acquired from domestic residents abroad minus income earned in the domestic market by foreigners.)

CHAPTER TWO

FROM FACTS TO PROBLEMS

Until now we established basic facts of urbanization relevant for middle-range planning. Indeed, trends until 2000 give a perspective of less than 20 years. We looked beyond the simple trend data and considered it in relation to other relevant data-types such as migration as a source of urbanization, economic development and housing.

In order to devise policy alternatives it is necessary to introduce a *normative* viewpoint which allows us to distinguish positive change from negative, progress from regress. On the other hand, for policy not all changes are of equal importance; processes which are at least partially conditioned by the authorities' action deserve special attention.

We assess the urbanization process in the interest of the *underpirvileged*. How does their situation develop and how can it be improved in absolute (time series) and relative (compared to the other social groups; e.g. relative pauperization) terms? Concerning the underprivileged, who sometimes need assistance, it is particularly appropriate to underline the fact that any human being is a conscious being. The underprivileged can be influenced by advice, yet only he finally determines what is for him a benefice. Equally, where possible, actions of underprivileged persons should not be replaced by the actions of the bureaucracy, transforming them into passive recipients.

As a reminder, we can sum up the most marked data features of Tropical Africa's urbanization process. We considered mainly 5 countries which have at least 10 million inhabitants: Nigeria (85 million inhabitants), Zaire (28), Tanzania (19), Kenya (16) and Ghana (12) — they make up more than half of Tropical Africa's population; also, large countries have different development profilse than small ones. Tropical Africa is one of the least urbanized regions of the world, although with a high inter-country variation (in Tropical Africa, Equatorial Guinea has the highest urbanization indicator 54% and Burundi the lowest 2.3%). For the period from independence until the end of the century the urbanization process has been and will be more rapid than that of the rest of the world. This cannot be attributed to the present low urbanization level because among the 5 countries, Zaire, which is already the most urbanized, also has the highest urbanization growth rate; this also means a further differentiation between rural and urbanized countries in Tropical Africa.

The main source of urbanization is the rural-urban migration but also the fact that age-specific survival rate in urban areas is better than in rural ones. Concerning the growth of the urban population, although the growth rate of Tropical Africa's population is one of the world's highest, (4% ~ 2% annual increase), the urban population increase rate is even twice as much, and 60% of this latter increase comes from the natural increase in urban areas, which is not the case in the developed world.

All major cities of the region (viz. with at least a million inhabitants) have a higher growth rate than the country's urban population. Thus the urban concentration predominates in the urbanization process. The metropoles (primate cities) "improve" their already pre-eminent position. (Only Zaire's two-city index decreases somewhat because of the exceptionally rapid increase in Kananga's population.) During the last 30 years of this century, Dar es Salaam grows with the fastest pace, but it is Zaire's urbanization which is of overwhelming interest. This country already has the highest urbanization indicator which also increases the most, and thus the country will be more than 50% urbanized in 2000. Its metropole, Kinshasa is the largest city of Tropical Africa and remains so despite the fact that Zaire is not the largest country and that its population growth rate is not the highest. In terms of economic capacity, among the 5 countries, Zaire also has the lowest GDP per capita and it has the highest overurbanization index as well as the highest urbanization overspeed index.

In 1970 more than half of the inhabitants of all large cities lived in slums and uncontrolled settlements in Tropical Africa, although we should consider the available data as unreliable and controversial (in terms of definition).

THE UNDERPRIVILEGED

The term "underprivileged" implies the absence of equal treatment. Equality, however, should not be understood as egalitarianism, which is for example, a numerically equal income for everybody (Ankerl 1978: 9–15). Equal treatment eliminates all aspects of a transaction which are formally irrelevant to it (Rawls). Commutative or exhange justice is best guaranteed if all parties in a transaction have equal bargaining power (Ankerl 1978: 20). However, for numerous reasons there is not a foolproof *procedure* to realize it in all situations. It would be clearly counterproductive to entertain the illusion that any constitution — Albanian, American, Chinese, Swiss or Tanzanian, etc. — can prevent situations where for deep historical, sociological and personal reasons the outcome of a transaction is systematically biased for some parties. It must be said in no less ambiguous terms that the differences in the possibilities to realize one's potentials in life do not always come from the imperatives of national production (namely the different collective utility of individuals) nor from the individual's own fault, but from arbitrariness. Basic societal theories to devise principles of social justice and corrective procedures for their day-to-day application have been dicsussed elsewhere (Ankerl 1978). Here we take a pragmatical approach.

We try to identify a set of persons, households or settings (neighborhoods), where a well-established systematic and persistent bias makes the individuals in these categories unable to defend their incontestably vital interests. The bias is systematic and persistent to such a point that the one-sided outcome of transactions cannot be redressed by chance *("hodie mihi, cras tibi")*.

In a society based on democratic legitimacy, underprivileged groups are often identified as "minoritites". What is meant by minorities? We stated (1978: 6–7):

> In the model of democracy the common good must serve every citizen equally. The substitution of majority rule for the absolute veto power of every citizen can only by justified on utilitarian grounds, in that it serves everyone more effectively in the long run. This alone gives its democratic legitimacy.
>
> The pragmatic advantage of majority rule is preserved only if the society preserves sufficient homogeneity so that every individual has an equal chance of being in the majority on a randomly chosen issue. If the society is sharply divided into distinct communities on religious, ethnic or regional grounds, then the mechanical and exclusive application of the one man, one vote rule will not insure the achievement of a democratic society based on a collective view of the common good.

If we now look for a net to save individuals from falling below a certain level in their existential struggle, it is not without interest to distinguish first two categories of negative discrimination (Ankerl 1965: 16–21):

1. *Disfunctional* discrimination's basic characteristic is that it also negatively affects the society's efficiency as a whole. (E.g., selecting candidates for higher education by their genealogical origin rather than by their

expected future performance, or hiring a less competent man for an engineering job rather than a more competent woman or a less competent pretty woman rather than a more competent unattractive one.)

2. *"Inhumane"* discrimination: while disfunctional discrimination is a concern for a country's economic policy, namely for its human resource management, this second category falls in another part of the societal policy (Ankerl 1978: 34, 48–51). Indeed, assistance to children and temporary unemployed can be justified on a purely economic basis, while the fate of the elderly, disabled persons and alike need the introduction of a comprehensive principle of justice, namely the acceptance of the principle that in a society each individual has an equal right to obtain the conditions of his happiness which are assured by the collectivity to its members. This is an all-embracing solidarity (Tévoédjrè 1976: 164–50). As we will see, solidarity does not develop spontaneously with the same intensity at all levels of mankind (world, nation, ethnic group, kinship, household) because in its most intensive form it implies the dissolution of the individual in a We-feeling, viz. one feels the other's suffering as his own (Ankerl 1980: 7).

This second category of justice includes persons without noticeable bargaining power, and the well-established strategy of societal policy must be designed in a manner that the most sensitive part of the redistribution is effectuated on the lowest possible level, where the solidarity feeling is actually intensive (families, for example). This also meets the requirements of the subsidiarity principle: redistribute on the lowest possible level where the charge is still bearable.

UNDERPRIVILEGE, AN ELUSIVE PHENOMENON

Underprivilege is easy to perceive in everyday life, but it eludes objective scientific definition. First, it has the tendency to play hide-and-seek with its synonyms, which change the question's emphasis: underprivileged, disadvantaged, discrimination (UN 1949), powerless, impoverished (pauperized), deprived (Stouffer), outcast. The enumeration is not exhaustive but already indicates essential aspects and alternative appearances of the phenomenon.

Underprivilege can be considered as a material aspect of life or can encompass immaterial aspects as well; it can be related to income or to resource in general (propertyless proletariat); income can be assessed in relation to need or to past income (absolute pauperism) or to other's income, "neighbor's", etc. (relative pauperization). Underprivilege can be apprehended not only on the income or input side (1), but also on the consumption side (2), and in so far as the consumption is a means to self-preservation, in terms of the state of the individuals themselves as the final output (3).

It will be the heuristic consideration which decides at which level the phenomenon can be effectively apprehended in developing countries without losing essential aspects.

Any income redistribution or public assistance is addressed to the needy. Any budget calculation based on need assessment requires a very complex model including hardly measurable variables (Ankerl 1965: 174 fig. and 197 fig.; 1978: 53s). Also, while individuals are the final consumers, in social reality the income recipient is actually the household.

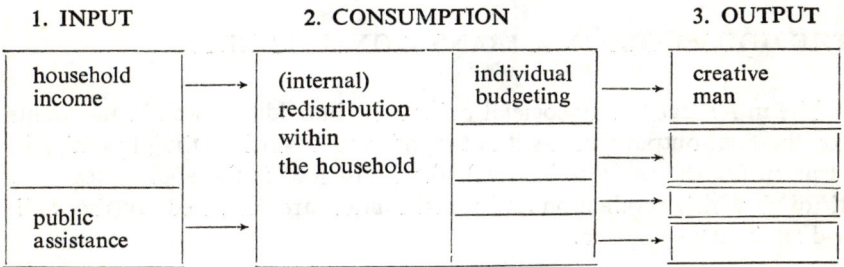

In order to assess competing claims, the income distribution cannot be referred to exclusively as the recipient's own assessment of his projects for self-fulfillment. A "just" interpersonal distribution of scarce resources cannot be conceived unless the authority formulates an idea of admissible goals of the different individuals. However, the authority (even if it will) can never completely circumvent the individual's autonomy by in-kind distribution because the individual can respond by waste. The only means to bridge the possible gap between the authority's norms and the individual's actual behavior is by the former's use of persuasion.

Interactive models including need assessment, multiple intervention (income assistance and persuasion), feedback and reevaluation are ready for experimentation; however, even in the United States, where very detailed and reliable survey and census data are available, experimental programs do not presently function in a satisfactory manner (Ankerl 1978: ch. VII).

In regions which are sparsely mapped by data a rougher approach is appropriate. One approach is to consider incremental income in relation to the notion of austerity. In this case, without making any sophisticated assumptions about needs of various social groups, the distributive authority tries to minimise waste (Ankerl 1978: 61–2, 79). The question to eb answered is the following: to which social categories should the next income increment be redirected (or simply the existing income transferred) in order to be used the most intensively for consumption? The roughest measure of wastage is that which is discarded to be picked up freely by others in the garbage. A next step is to learn by survey what budget item will increase in case of income augmentation (food, etc.). Indeed, the urgency of a need is revealed by the readiness to make sacrifices for its satisfaction — either renouncing another budget item or working more.

After income as input (1) and consumption (2) (Tobin), others advocate an approach which is concerned above all with variables on the output level (3) such as life expectancy (Morris: 20).

THE HOUSEHOLD IN A TRANSITIONAL SOCIETY

While in respect to any societal policy, the individual's well-being counts for the final output (just as it is the individual which is the physical substratum for the most solid data), the household is the sociological unit through which production and redistribution are mediated to the individual for consumption.

Through the transformation of the functions and composition of the family, the household remains the basic common unit in society. It is first of all a budget-hsaring unit which thus has redistributive functions, but it is also a prime sociological reality which involves a shared habitat with its regular face-to-face communication. By fixing this essential characteristic, the household concept encompasses the nuclear family, the extended family or even a whole compound (concerning the census of 1961 in Benin, it is called a "houseful"; Laslette: 28, 36–8) or on the contrary, includes a single person or two people who, for example, double up in a slum (*UN Patterns*:... 94–7). Kenya's Central Bureau of Census defined in 1977 the household in the following terms (Casley: 187):

> Household is a person or group of persons normally living together under one roof or several roofs within the same compound or homestead area and sharing a community of life by their dependence on common holding as a source of income and food, which normally but not necessarily involves them in eating from a 'common pot'.

How does the household-concept as a budget-sharing unit apply to the rural and urban underprivileged for comparison in a transitional society?

Schematizing in bipolar terms, in the traditional subsistence economy (chiefly pastoral and agrarian), the household was necessarily a family — embedded in a larger kinship network. It was also a complete productive unit which mainly distributed and consumed their own products among themselves.

The passage from this small-scale community-oriented local farming economy into a large-scale mainly market-oriented money economy — in many parts of Africa the use of money was entirely unknown until two decades ago (Little 1974: 107) — removes the organization of the economic life from the household. The household becomes a simple redistributer between wage earner and dependents as well as a place of economical joint consumption. By frequent individual migration chiefly from smaller rural settlements to larger and larger urban ones, the family-based household is replaced by a more or less fortuitous sharing arrangement among individuals without clearly delineated kinship structure.

Transition always means coexistence of old, new and hybrid forms. Indeed, at the present time we cannot assess the situation of individuals in the various households in Tropical Africa exclusively in terms of monetary income. All calculation based exclusively on taxable household income earned on the formal labor market and recorded by the National Accounts disregards non-negligible incomes in two respects.

1. The traditional farming household preserves important functions mainly in rural areas, with considerable self-consumption.

2. On the marge of large-scale enterprises with formal organization an informal or quartenary sector mushrooms with untaxed earners — small earners, yet earners. This same phenomenon is also present in the crisis-ridden economies of the industrialized countries with do-it-yourself and "moonlighting" of ths "unemployed", but the magnitude of this non-organized and largely ignored sector has a smaller proportion than in Tropical Africa's transitional societies (Ankerl 1984: 44–5).

DIFFERENTIATING RURAL AND URBAN UNDERPRIVILEGED

We recall that our task here cannot be to handle the issue of the underprivileged in its broadest meaning. Neither do we handle here the lot of the underprivileged in Tropical Africa in absolute terms, nor do we compare theirs ituation to others living in other social systems such as those which prevail, for example, in Western Europe. We look only at the question of how the urbanization process affects the extent and degree of underprivilege and whether the effects are positive or negative. Effects of the urbanization process must also be differentiated according to its speed and direction (metropolitan agglomeration or middle and small towns). Among the underprivileged one should distinguished between urban natives and urban immigrants (nationals and foreigners). (Ankerl 1974: 582.)

Even if we narrow the problem of the underprivileged to a comparison between rural and urban inhabitants within the framework of a given society, the problem remains complex on still other levels, such as the identification of the person and the forms of underprivilege. Because of the mainly subsistence economy of rural areas and the more monetary character of urban economy, it is difficult to find instruments to measure and monitor urban and rural deprivation with equal accuracy.

Individuals subject to negative discrimination can be (from the viewpoint of social statistics) identified as members of a group or inhabitants of an area (ghetto) in so far as this area is homogenous enough (Guy Bernard; Gibbal). Census data are based on households, therefore we can distinguish underprivileged households and underprivileged persons within the household. As we indicated already, people with little or no bargaining power or no assets to trade are exposed foremostly to material discrimination, although in different forms and emphases in rural community and urban society.

Elderly and disabled persons do not have the capacity to satisfy their needs for daily survival (subsistence). The Spartan society, for example, disposed of handicapped infants by pushing them down the mountain Taygetus. Whereas elderly persons may have previously earned assets, those who are disabled by birth will not. They cannot even promise future services for credit because they will have a negative balance for the rest of their lives (Ankerl 1965: 10, fig., 165; 1978: 45–51). In the traditional rural community family ties address this problem because a household is never formed by a single person. Of course, discretionary power of the family is here nearly complete.

Infants are also physically and mentally dependent for the satisfaction of their daily needs, but they have a much better social "credit rating" than the resourceless elderly, because they can trade their future work force as an asset (Ankerl 1965: 21, fig. 1; 1978: 34).

We see that a lack of bargaining power to establish a reciprocally useful social relationhsip can either come from inborn or acquired defects (e.g.r by accident), or only from the natural life cycle (to be "under age" o, "aged").

Other sources of underprivilege have only biological connotation but it is truly the arbitrary interpretation attributed to biological characteristics by social prejudice which creates the disadvantaged status. Such is the lot of the "weaker sex" in a patriarchal society (and vice versa).

Physically able and mentally sound adults can fall into a disadvantaged situation by lack of access to means and resources to use their working capacities. We find landless laborers, smallholders, rural artisans (Scott 1981: 46–7), and unemployed in the cities. While the problem of the elderly and the disabled is statistically contained, unemployment can reach uncontrolled proportions because of the lack of economic organization in a society, creating a societal crisis.

Having enumerated these underprivileged situations, we also learn that they are not disconnected cases distributed by chance but constitute coherent series of life situations which begin for all individuals before birth. These unfortunate situations have cumulative characters and the person himself becomes underprivileged and not only his momentaneous situation. Genealogy and neighborhood give the intergenerational and "geographical" context. These circumstances determine which of the person's capacities and aspirations will be developed by education (i.e., socialization in general). In the village community social problems are addressed characteristically at a local level with relatively strong distinctions between underprivileged households and underprivileged individuals within the households where the latter is not a community but a family concern, while in urban agglomerations this distinction is less pronounced.

We discussed mainly the material aspects of underprivilege. This is one angle. There are other forms of disadvantage in the transitional African societies. Indeed, we have alreadys een in European history that Jews, for example, in the past often had large fortunes, but they were denied access to some institutions by statutory presciption, or that in India wealthy untouchables suffer from discrimination or that wealthy blacks are discriminated against in South Africa. This kind of nonfinancial disadvantage is a very important point if we compare rural and urban underprivileged because this phenomenon has a very different form in subsistence and money economies.

MEASURING AND MONITORING THE UNDERPRIVILEGED'S SITUATION

The underprivileged's situation can be characterized by an insufficient access to necessary goods and services. Subjectively, the individual is frustrated by the lack of the development of his talent or the use of his potentials, and because his aspirations are beyond his reach. Objectively in so far as the able-bodied persons are concerned, the country's manpower as a human resource is lost. Measuring and monitoring this situation in rural and urban areas is a very complicated task. We can do it either on the input side or on the output side. We can either show the person's lack of means, or his resulting poor physiological and mental state.

As a matter of fact, in a given social context and at a given level of scientific knowledge, we can approximate in physical terms which lack of need-satisfactions will certainly have a negative effect on the individual's state as a living being. This is the lowest floor for basic need (Ankerl 1978: 53–61). FAO focused its interest on rural areas — where agriculture is predominent — and made detailed studies about components of living conditions (FAO: *Essentials of Rural Welfare*, Rome, 1949). Beyond household income and possessions, type of house, furnishing, sanitation electricity, protected drinking water, food consumption, clothing, shoes, education (literacy and numeracy), transport, communication, health service, recreational facilities are described (Scott 1981: 42, Drewnowski 1970, both working for the UN Research Institute for Social Development, UNRISD in Geneva.)

Without translating physical magnitudes into monetary aggregates, privileged and underprivileged are globally incomparable just as overall progress in time cannot be measured. Indeed, resourceless situations of a group can result either from the fact that they are in a low-income country (which can reflect an underprivileged situation of the country on an international level) or because of the inequality of income in the country. General level of living can be apprehended by aggregating the household budget either in monetary income or in expediture. Comparing rural and urban situations in a transitional society, where few economic processes are controlled by the market by receiving a price in monetary terms, is a very risky undertaking. As we already noted, many processes are outside the National Accounts.

ILO focuses its attention especially on the regular employment in the non-agricultural sector, particularly in urban settings. But with this approach we should add to the income, self-consumption, do-it-yourself in free time, income from the informal sector (also barter services as gifts) and free or highly subsidized public services. And yet in a society with little industrialization these estimated components of the income are very important as well as very different in urban and rural areas, and their estimation cumbersome and often arbitrary. On the expenditure side, theoretically we have income after deduction of tax and savings. However, pricing home-grown products can be problematical in conditions where there are few sales, or where local prices vary according to the region of the country. Of course, in case of a survey, if the income is not taxed there is no guaranty about the veracity of the household's statements (Scott: 32).

Due to the cumbersomeness of the calculation as well as uncertainties in the results, instead of calculating all components, dominant items of the underprivileged budget are used as indicators. We know for example, that in developing countries over 70% of expenses goes for food, but that this proportion declines visibly and continously with improvement in the household's situation. Therefore, if the proportion is known, it indicates the level of living; if the expense for food is known, we can also estimate approximately the magnitude of nonfood items (Altimir O. and J. Sourouille; J. Bukh; F. Lisk). The dwelling of a household gives a very integrated and palpable indication of the living conditions (UN Economic Commission for Africa).

SOCIETAL INDICATORS

For our purposes, indicators or indexes (composite indicators) must show first of all that the well-being of the population as a whole makes progress in so far as this well-being depends on the country's economic and social policy. We look also for indicators which are useful for policy making and which can be used for objective goal targeting and for evaluation of performances (performance auditing). This indicator or index must not show only the mean or median but also how the well-being of the population is distributed on the whole, especially for underprivileged rural and urban populations. Of course, subjective satisfaction depends upon expectation and only very distantly on policy. Subjective satisfaction is also a very unstable state. Happiness of various persons can be even less meaningful totalized in statistics. Therefore, well-being as a function of policy measures must be measured in objective terms (Carley, Morris). Policy goals are reached when the means necessary to well-being are at the individual's disposal — otherwise, freedom of choice cannot be recognized. This is one of the very reasons that, where possible, cash assistance coupled with advice is preferable to in-kind help (Ankerl 1965: 199–216; 1978: 63–72). Thus, the final outcome of this kind of measure depends on the individual's use of his cash allowance.

Objectives of any societal policy are based on value order considered consensual (Ankerl 1965: 40). For the economic good of the society, the development and maintenance of the value of the population (also called human resource) are such objective sespecially for the developing countries

(Ankerl 1965: 61). Theoretically, we can express this value by the median (or mean) length of the active life multiplied by the average I.Q. calculated according to the total number of conceived human beings (Ankerl 1965: 54); thus this index reflects a part of longevity, the number of abortions, stillbirth, infant death rate, morbidity and mental capacities. However, it has two handicaps: (a) it is difficult to operationalize and (b) the well-being of elderly persons is not directly integrated. Indeed, it does not measure goals of societal policy in general, but only those of economic policy. On the other hand, it would be ill-advised to replace in this index, for societal policy purposes, the active life by longevity or life expectancy; indeed it is a consensus that prolongation of active life is a goal superceding that of life in short (Morris: 31).

We now look for operational indicators which best circumscribe this long-term outlook of the societal policy. We look also for indicators which inform the public and the authorities what progress has been made for conditions which affect the realization of societal policy goals (Carley: 27, 45). These latter analytical indicators consider the various inputs and can be disaggregated according to the specific issues for groups or areas (intra-urban, inter-urban indicators (Carley: 130s). We mentioned the "professional biases" of the different specialized international organizations in the measurement of development. FAO uses indicators which show food consumption and production, ILO considers primarily formal industrial employment and the World Bank (IBRD) uses global data from National Accounts (*GNP* or *GDP* or *MPS*) without much interest in non-monetary economic process. WHO approaches societal goals by "vital statistics" and finally UNICEF, with its new director (1980), James Grant, tried to synthesize WHO goals concerning infant mortality (1) and life expectancy at age one (2) with the UNESCO goal concerning literacy (3) in an index called *PQLI — Physical Quality of Life Index*. These three composing indicators are scaled — which is in itself an implicit weighting for policy purposes — and summed up with equal weight (33% for each one) (Morris: 48).

This index or at least its composing indicators merit special attention and critical evaluation. We see immediately that on the one hand, diminishing infant mortality and increasing life expectancy are certainly essential elements of societal policy goals (even if their relative significance to other objectives such as morbidity, etc. is questionable) and the literacy itself can reflect some cultural biases (Scribner; P. L. Knox 1978: "Composite measures are pitfalls of cultural imperialism"), and that on the other hand, this index is very sensitive to income distribution; viz. this index shows the strongest improvement if the societal policy concentrates its effort on the most underprivileged group, and this is especially true for the less developed countries.

Let us now see what the technical requirements are for a well-conceived and well-formulated indicator and index. Of course, the emphasis on one or another aspects depends on the purpose of the indicator: measuring trends and progress for performance auditing (input/output, social accounting, monitoring social change; Sheldon: 693), comparing situations across jurisdictions with similar characteristics (e.g., determining neediness for international aid) or comparing operational units for their efficiency.

OECD (1979; Glatzer: 9) makes an inventory of data sources for 32 selected social indicators and evaluates them for their

1. validity,
2. reliability,
3. sensitivity and
4. comparability.

The Urban Institute (Harty) in Washington D. C. posits 6 very practical criteria for the selection of performance indicators:

1. Appropriateness and validity (objective conformity, minimizing detrimental effects).
2. Uniqueness, accuracy and reliability (avoiding overlapping, double counting — except for testing the measures themselves).
3. Completeness and comprehensibility (cover the desired objective and be understandable).
4. Controllability (conditions measured must be at least partially under government control).
5. Cost (staff and data collection cost must be reasonable).
6. Feedback time (information available within time-frame necessary for decision-making).

The UN Research Institute for Social Development (UNRISD) enumerates 7 criteria (McGranahan: 6–7) for comparative indicators:

1. Conceptual significance (indicate a significant aspect of development).
2. Validity (Conceptual and statistical validity — indicate what it is intended to measure).
3. Discriminative power (distinguish effectively between developing countries at different levels).
4. Comparability (operationally defined to measure the same thing in different countries).
5. Quality of data (collected by adequate means, are consistent with each other, complete and otherwise reliable).

6. Availability of data (sufficient number of countries have the data).
7. Sectoral balance in the set of indicators and avoidance of duplication.

The Overseas' Development Council posits 6 criteria for the construction of a relevant composite measure of international socioeconomic performance (Morris has here *PQLI* in mind, p. 21; see also Drewnowski for a composite indicator):

1. It must not assume that there is only one possible pattern of development.
2. Avoid standards that reflect the values of specific societies.
3. Measure results, not input.
4. Reflect distribution of social results.
5. Be simple to construct and easy to comprehend.
6. Lend itself to international comparison.

In order to measure societal progress in a cardinal manner by an index (viz. composite indicator), the authority, as we have already mentioned, should have a consensual value order which allows him to place in precise quantitative relations all non-negligible aspects of this progress which can be influenced by policy. Of course, there cannot be any measurement without availability of statistically acceptable data for a reasonable cost within operationally relevant time (or at least indications that these data can be generated if the authority so decides).

We should evaluate PQLI in light of these criteria. Let us first look at the three components:

1. *Longevity* is certainly a generally accepted goal, and as an average, it can be better measured by life expectancy than by simple death rate statistics which depend upon age composition of the population (Morris: 38). It is also a useful idea to indicate life expectancy at age one because in this manner it is independent from the infant mortality which is calculated under age one. However, it should be noted that on the level of vital values, the absence of morbidity is also, for many, an equally valuable goal; therefore, in this respect, the expectancy of the duration of active (creative) life is the cardinal measure from the viewpoint of the individual's physical well-being as well as that of the economy. Yet, in so far as the high or low priority of this goal, there is not a consensus among all *weltanschauungs* and societies (Western countries, low-income tropical countries, etc.). In fact, longevity obviously concerns more the quantity of life than its quality.

2. Lowering *infant mortality* is also a generally acceptable goal but its priority among other goal resmains disputable.

3. Finally, *literacy* as a component of the Physical Quality of Life Index is not a physical aspect at all (Morris: 3) and its measurement is not easy. To give it priority among the various mental aspects of societal process is arbitrary and without doubt culturally biased.[1] (Its significance is different in rural and urban areas, etc.) Remaining on the socioeconomic level, *numeracy* is certainly not a less desirable measure of mental progress (and functional competency an even more desirable one). Clearly, literacy can only be a policy target in the less developed countries.

Concerning the *PQLI* itself, not only is the weighting of its 3 components arbitrary, but the scaling of each component itself has been made on an intuitive basis (Morris: 41, 44, 49).

In summing up, we can say that the components of *PQLI* are interesting indicators for assessing societal progress, if and where these data are available in a reliable manner, or at least producible (Morris: 34). The composite indicator itself (*PQLI*) reflects an arbitrarily quantified value hierarchy; neither can it be considered an expression of highest priority which must guide policy decision in every society. (It is not a universal "pan-human index". Morris: 21). As literacy cannot be a surrogate for all aspects of mental development (Morris: 3), the implicit contention to be an "inexpensive surrogate for adjusted *GNP*" (Morris: 56) is inconsistent with the *PQLI's* profile itself (Morris: 13) and this contention is inappropriate.

Especially for the less developed countries, viz., with low *GNP* per capita, the 3 components of the index are good evaluators in order to learn how the benefits of economic progress are shared by the whole population which also includes the poorest stratum. As a matter of fact, the improvement of these 3 indicators cannot be pursued efficiently by the government unless it concentrates its efforts on the underprivileged. (Cf. *DRR=Disparity Reduction Rate,* Morris: 60.) This is the strong point of these indicators. It is an unfortunate paradox that just where these indicators are the most useful — in the less developed countries — the data are seldom reliably available. (According to the UNRISD data bank for 120 countries, data about infant mortality are available in 65 countries, about life expectancy in 76 countries and about literacy in 65.) Of course, the reliability of the data varies a great deal (McGranahan: 19). Concerning the composite indicator itself, it is interesting to study the coefficient of association (e.g., Tschuprow's) or correlation between the components (McGranahan: 8; Scott: 42; Cole: 121: Correlation Matrix), but it is a vain effort to combine them according to the precise weighting to become a unique measure for societal programs. *PQLI* cannot replace the *GNP* per capita, but must be qualified as has been done by its conceptualizer himself (Kuznets), as well as by critics. (J. Tobin: 512, underlines that consumption statistics are more important than production statistics for measuring socioeconomic progress.)

INDICATORS AND THE UNDERPRIVILEGED IN URBAN AND RURAL AREAS

The underprivileged is a person who is an "underachiever" in the realization of his potentials because of his disadvantaged status in his society. In his exchange with his non-human (physical) environment, the society's economic organization does not give him a sufficient share in the national production to avoid deprivation or even starvation, and its societal organization — by statutory or other means — can also deprive him from meaningful reciprocal exchange. Causes of discrimination can be very diverse (lack of household or personal income, of public services, "derogatory" social status); yet, variation in basic health indicators such as infant mortality and life expectancy (at age one), and basic socialization indicators (schooling) according to households grouped by income, geographical areas or the main earner's profession are significant to apprehend the phenomenon empirically.

As we know, it is appropriate to express social phenomena by quantitative data when the researcher has a precise idea of why, what and how to measure. It is also advisable to relate the researched phenomena to data which are already at our disposal before we make costly proposals for new data collection, especially if we have clear indications about the data's reliability. We present all available data for the concerned regions and countries in table 9.

Infant mortality data are available from 1970 for 65 countries among 120 having more than one million inhabitants (UNRISD data bank; McGranahan: 7, 19). (Of course, for measuring performance, data must be available periodically in regular intervals for local areas and groups.)

Life expectancy data has the advantage of easy understandability. The availability of data (76 countries) as well as its varying reliability are similar to those concerning infant mortality. The problem is that, in most of the cases, available data concern life expectancy at birth, and thus overlap infant mortality. (The negative correlation between life expectancy at birth and infant mortality, -0.96 (McGranahan: 8) or -0.98 (Cole: 123), is quasi-tautological and uninformative.) To make comparisons, either we use life expectancy at birth data as a general indicator and use the infant mortality data as its analytical sub-indicator (for learning more

TABLE 9.

Average Per Capita GDP, Life Expectancy, Illiteracy Rate and PQLI

Country	GDP per capita $		Infant mortality (per 1000 live births)			Life expectancy at birth (years)				Illiteracy rate			PQLI	
	1970	1979 or 1978	1960	1975	1978	1960	1975	1979	Δ between 1960 and 1979	1970	1979	Δ between 1970 and 1979	1960	1970s
Zaire	90	220	–	160	–	40	44	47	7	57.1	42.1	−15.0	–	32
Tanzania	100	260	–	162	–	42	44	52	10	63.1	52.5	−10.6	–	31
Kenya	140	370	126	119	91	41	50	55	14	68.6	50.4	−18.3	37	39
Nigeria	140	730	–	180	–	39	38?	49	10	76.0	70.1	− 5.9	–	25
Ghana	260	900	141	156	–	40	48	49	9	69.5	55.2	−14.3	–	35

The table shows all data available for the 5 countries.

Sources: – *World Development Report 1981*
– *UN World Statistics in Brief 1980*
– *1980 World Bank Atlas*
– *1977 World Data Sheet*, Population Reference Bureau, Inc. Washington D. C
– Morris
– Cole

about causes and devising policy), or we convert the at-birth data into at-age-one data as required by the *PQLI*.

Literacy (over age 15) data are only significant in the broader context of socialization as a preparation (schooling) and initiation into a specific role in a given society (Scribner; Paige). Besides the problem of its conceptual validity, reliable data gathering is also very problematical. As noted, some data do not count any other language knowledge or sign system than the "Western" phonemic alphabet as literacy (Vai script learned in Liberian families, or even Arabic). On the other hand, literacy is a gradual concept: there are people who can read but not write or who can write only a certain number of words ("semi-literate", Little 1965: 5). (Scott of UNRISD reported that 60% of the people interviewed in Jamaica claimed to be literate but only 40% passed the test. We experienced in Abidjan that many people's literacy stops at the level needed to read and fill out a Toto or Lotto pool coupon.) We note that the UNRISD data bank (McGranahan: 19) has literacy data from 65 countries (and enrollment in elementary and secondary education data from 99 countries). After all the reserves expressed about literacy data, it is comforting to learn that the literacy rate is highly correlated to the other *PQLI* data: -0.91 to infant mortality and $+0.93$ to life expectancy at birth (McGranahan: 8); therefore, one of the other data-type can serve in the case of necessity as a surrogate for the other as a societal indicator.

Average infant mortality, life expectancy and illiteracy rates vary strongly according to regions, countries, urban and rural areas and household groups (Morris: 134; Cole: 102). While some variations in health statistics (e.g., life expectancy) concerning male and female have a genetic explanation (Bogue: 585), the other variations do not. There is a positive correlation between average income (*GDP* per capita) and average *PQLI*, but not as strong as we could expect (Morris: 65 fig. 2). Within a country's population for which the *GDP* per capita is calculated, the performance in *PQLI* depends on how widely the *GDP* is distributed (how much it reaches the low-income population) and on how this income is used. If the *GDP* reflects the performance of the economic policy of a country, income redistribution and the income's use in specific consumption are questions of social policy. We can observe that infant survival, life expectancy and literacy rate can be improved in low-income countries by increasing the *GDP* and especially by enlarging the low-income stratum's share of the *GDP*.

In Chenery's book (p. 8–9), we find a survey of 17 countries in the 1960's (Chad, Niger, Senegal and Zambia are included from Africa) concerning the percentage of *GNP* going to the poorest 40% of households. (See also *World Development Report 1983:* table 27.) While the *GNP* per capita for the 17 countries varies between 529 and 97 dollars, the poorest household's share is between 20.4% and 6.5% of the *GNP*. We can theorize that the *GDP* per capita multiplied by the percentage of income going to the *poorest 40% of households* is a better predictor of the country's performance concerning longevity, infant mortality and literacy than the *GDP* per capita alone (i.e. the measure of spread is as important as the average income, Morris: 73).

A second important variable determining the performance in *PQLI* is the part of income distributed in the form of free or highly subsidized public services. This should be especially counted in the calculation of the low-income strata because they are usually the biggest beneficiaries; also, it is important that some goods and services are distributed in kind (e.g., health services, medical facilities, pipe-borne water, sewage) because these measures allow the application of the newest scientific findings (e.g., in medical science) to be spread rapidly to the largest possible segment of the population. In China, for example, because of considerable regional variations, the share of the 40% poorest households is not higher than 18% of the *GNP*. China increased the average life expectancy at birth between 1950 and 1970 from 36 years to 64, while the low-income countries in the world improved from 37 to only 51 years, and even the middle-income countries improved from 48 years to only 61. Indeed, the highly subsidized basic education, nutrition and health programs available to everybody free of charge diminished especially the infant mortality (*World Development...: 101*).

In our table 9, we presented the health and literacy data which are available for the 5 largest countries of Tropical Africa. Even if we clearly designated the social policy (income redistribution and public services) as responsible for the development of *PQLI*, namely a country can over or under perform in relation to its economic means (*GDP* per capita), we must be very cautious in judging the different governments' performances in Tropical Africa. In reality there are historical reasons for the discrepancies between *GDP* per capita and *PQLI* in different countries. In fact, these countries were decolonized less than three decades ago and the different colonial powers exercised very different policies: some concentrated on the development of an elite, others addressed the well-being of the average native peoples or completely neglected the "population in the bush". Therefore, the interesting and relevant data for judging the social development in relation to economic development *(GDP)* is not the inter-country comparison but the time series: how much is the improvement of *GDP* per capita followed by the improvement in infant survival and life expectancy? And yet, as we can see in table 9, we lack reliable data taken in regular intervals and therefore trends and progress cannot be assessed. (Perhaps Kenya is an exception.)

If we now assess the underprivileged's situation in rural and urban areas by using the *PQLI* differences as an indication, we find data for Tropical Africa only for Ghana and Liberia (Morris: 91).

PQLI in the 1970's

	Rural	Urban	Urban superiority in %
Ghana	28	54	93
Liberia	27	42	56

This shows a net advantage for the urban population. Basta (p. 113–24) states that infant mortality and illiteracy rates are lower in urban than in rural areas.[2] Most of the data are not reliable (especially in rural areas; Carley) and often undifferentiated between metropolis and smaller agglomerations in urban areas.

In order to devise the most appropriate policy for improving the underprivileged's situation in a country, let us see how the question is differently addressed in rural and in urban areas, and which policy measures are the most specifically appropriate.

PUBLIC SERVICES IN URBAN AND RURAL AREAS

By definition, an urban area is characterized by a relatively large number of people living (and congregating) on a relatively small territory.

In principle, health services (better medical facilities), sanitation (protected pipe-borne water), electricity, transporation, good educational facilities and cultural amenities (quality entertainment) can be provided in urban settings with better cost-effectiveness because of the economies of scale. For a developing country with particularly scarce resources, this is a non-negligible concern in the planning of its expenditures, and since public services are usually subsidized or free of charge, and largely used by the underprivileged, the benefit goes to them. For this reason, it is irresponsible to speak thoughtlessly about "urban bias" (Lipton). We should recall how the quality of all public services deteriorated in Democratic Kampuchea, where cities were systematically emptied.

Yet these advantages of urban life can be effective only under determined circumstances:

1. Urban density cannot be understood exclusively in terms of land use (built/unbuilt land) but in terms of human density, such as residential density (number of inhabitants/ha). To assure this higher density by

multistoried buildings is a typical feature of urban living (Ankerl 1974: 578; 1978: 387; 1983: 82). And yet, societies with strong pastoral and agricultural traditions are habituated to single-story living. "Horizontal living" has deep roots in Africa (Fapohunda: 46), even if we should correct the widely held idea that Africa does not have urban traditiosn (Fassassi: 21, 97, 99, 123; e.g. Tombouctou in Mali).

However, there is no way to disregard the equation:
residential density or population density (total number of residents per total territory)$=(b \times c)/a$, where
$a=$dwelling surface in m² per inhabitant,
$b=$built land/total land,
$c=$weighted average number of stories of buildings.

Indeed, for urban settlements, a high residential density is required, and there are only 3 possible choices: either crowded apartments (see a) or lack of green surfaces (a high value for b) or higher buildings (c). No other solution is possible. Therefore, any attempt to create urban density (which is necessary for the advantageous delivery of public services) without high-rise buildings in African neighborhoods would either deprive the city of green surfaces or create overcrowded dwellings. (In Abidjan for example, Treichville, the popular neighborhood, has a residential density of around 200 inhabitants/ha, and Port-Bouet a little more. These are not high densities but the land is nearly completely covered by single-floor housing.)

Neither the experts nor the authorities are responsible for making choices for people, but what they can do is enlarge the range of choice by imaginative thinking and point to the alternatives where choices must be made. And it is up to the authority to explain the situation to the people. It must be said in no ambiguous terms that advantages cannot be infinitely cumulated. For a long time it has been asserted by so-called "ecology experts", that garden cities can exist without high-rise buildings and that village life is possible in the city. However, if the average citizen has his villa — or family cottage — in the center, then there is no longer any downtown. The extended city of urban-living villagers cannot deliver its mentioned advantages.

2. In terms of dynamics, the population increase of a certain urban settlement should be checked and held within a calculable speed which takes into account the city's immediate natural and rural environment and the public facilities' maximal capacities; otherwise, the quality and extent of the public services deteriorate and especially the underprivileged will suffer from the reduced services. Beyond the natural growth of the urban

population, as we will see later, migration must not only be contained quantitatively but also guided qualitatively. It is not indifferent to the cities' good functioning which direction the rural-urban migration takes (middle-size city with free capacities or already overcrowded metropolis) nor how stable the population is. Transient remigrants implies additional public expenditures (integration, etc.) without any expected returns (cf. circular migration).

3. In intra-urban terms, a judicious urban policy requires that public services have an appropriate spatial distribution (i.e., spread over neighborhoods). *Small Area Statistics* (Carley: 141s) show how this distribution is realized. Service should be concentrated, where it is most intensively used, and subsidized according to need assessment. (E.g., subsidy for basic public services in populous neighborhoods but only incentives for the maintenance of a quality theater.) M. Cohen (p. 57) evokes an interesting example from Abidjan:

> Whereas Cocody has a large number of health and welfare services for its well-off residents, the quartiers populaires of Treichville, Adjamé, and Nouveau Koumassi provide barely minimal services for their much larger populations ... the new eight story, 500-bed Centre Hospitalier Universitaire, one of the largest and most modern hospitals in all of Africa, was built in Cocody ... While permitting easy access for the residents of Cocody, the hospital is linked to the rest of the city by a single, overcrowded bus line.

(We note that in the last years a rapid new bus service was introduced in Abidjan.)

HOUSING

The habitat of the underprivileged allows us to assess his situation in the most thorough manner. However, the danger here is to make this evaluation with the indicators used for European countries where frost and the climatic conditions in general do not allow outdoor living. The evaluation of the housing conditions is even more subjectivistic if the "Western expert" evaluates the housing requirements necessary for his adaptation to the tropics. The most pertinent assessment results from a comparison between urban and rural housings. In this case we compare 2 settings with a similar climate and ethnic context.

Housing can be evaluated in relation to its characteristics: number and size of the rooms (in relation to the number of occupants), their arrangement (e.g., access to the kitchen), their relation to the atmospherics pace (one- or multi-storied building), their insulation (against rain and heat) and their equipment (electricity, drinking-water supply, sewage) (Ankerl 1981 and 1983).

According to the UN Economic Commission for Africa (p. 21), we dispose of data for ten countries in Tropical Africa. Around 1960, Tropical Africa's housing was characterized by the predominance of one-room dwellings (more than half of all dwellings). The average number of persons per room varied between 1.5 (for the city of Dakar) and 3.4 (for C.A.R.). In order to evaluate the underprivileged's situation, it would be more important to know not only the average number of rooms but also how this varies by neighborhood. Sampling surveys and case studies tell us more about the slums. Fapohunda (p. 39) reports, for example, that in the Sabongari sector of Kano, Nigeria, the occupancy is 7 persons per room (cf. Schwertfeger).

This situation can be evaluated in light of the life-style prevailing on an African compound. Concerning one-storied housing, the actual occupancy of the rooms is the relevant data; namely if the season allows, life goes on outside around the fireplace as a cooking place, and only during the night and in the rainy season is the dwelling occupancy complete (Fassassi: 13–4). On the other hand, the kitchen, whether outside or inside, is a central gathering place; therefore, a kitchen which is large by European standards (20 m^2) is small by African ones, not only as a function of the different family size but also because of the more community-oriented life style and the daily gathering of relatives. The roof is also an important aspect of a dwelling: the traditional thatched roof has to be replaced every two years. A more appropriate roof has not yet been invented. The corrugated sheets are not a solution because of their poor heat insulation. (Hot humid zone and hot dry zone should be differentiated. Ankerl 1983: 87–90.) Concerning the heat, for people born in the tropical climate, air-conditioning is not a necessity, and good ventilation is acceptable and even preferred.

For urban dwellings, better equipment is one of the most important ways to compensate for the lack of the favorable natural environment which benefits the housing in rural settings. And yet, the mushrooming uncontrolled settlements often lack a drinking-water supply or a well with safe water because of the high level of ground water. They may also lack sewage and drainpipes, thus, in the rainy season, the houses often have 20–30 cm of high ground water in the rooms (e.g., in Port-Bouet, Abidjan).

As we already evoked in the previous section, a broader problem appears here – an urbanistic one: the city loses its economic advantage if it must assure the public services for a large population which refuse to live in multistoried buildings. Moreover, if the one-storied arrangement is generally used in a densely populated city, the city will lose all its green surfaces. (Of course, the population's acceptance of extremely high room occupancy, i.e., only a few m² per person in the dwelling, somewhat diminishes the urge for high-rise construction.) We have already mentioned in the previous section the 3 alternatives from among which the choice could and must be made. If at least the downtown population in Africa accepts the multistoried dwellings, it means that the apartment's spaciousness must be greater because of the absence of outdoor living. The multistoried urban housing in Tropical Africa should not follow the European arrangements (lack of terraces, balconies, etc.). The solutions are yet to be developed by African architects such as Fassassi and Fathy.

In the present phase of development, progress for improved sanitation and public services could be made without causing unbearable expenditures for the collectivity by adding a new floor to the single-storied houses instead of extending horizontally the urban sprawl (Ankerl 1983: 88).

FOOD SUPPLY

In developings countrie, 70–80% of the household budget goes for food. Food supply is an especially important problem in Sub-Saharan Africa, where in 1984, 21 countries had critical food shortages (FAO). Besides South Asia, this region is the only one where the food grain consumption per capita decreased between 1970/3 and 1976/9. (According to the *World Development Report...*: 191–4, for the low-income countries this decrease was 0,5% between 1961/1964 and 1970/1973 and 1,2% between 1970/1973 and 1976/1979.) Another significant fact is that in relation to this region, the export and import of agricultural products increased since 1973.

Paradoxical as it is, we can read in many psublication that the food supply in urban areas is often better than in rural ones. It is well-known that for the profitable production and distribution of non-agricultural products, the production's location is determined more by the location of the market, labor force and the supplying industry than by the location of the natural resources. The labor force in agriculture and the percentage of population in rural areas are highly correlated. (According to Cole it is +0.92.) Cities are not self-sufficient in agricultural products. Although it cannot be stated in general terms that cities have a better food supply (Newland: 11), it is incontestable that they have a mores table food supply than rural areas. This is a dramatic fact for the underprivileged because in the case of small-holdings using a very rudimentary agrotechnique and operating without stock, the seasonal variation (e.g., the period before the crop) and crop failure can especially affect the nutrition of children, pregnant and nursing mothers and signify hardship and even starvation (Tévoédjrè 1981: 41). The lack of investment and ill-advised investment in rural areas explains this paradoxical situation. A metropolitan and multinational bias appears. Fapohunda states (p. 36):

> Marketing boards in Nigeria and Ghana, for example, accumulated large reserves of funds by paying the farmers less than the world market prices for their export crops.

In order to employ the whole rural population, more investment is necessary in these areas in general, but the expansion of the agricultural products aimed for export (viz., for the world market), has a negative side: the internal food demands is not directly covered, and instead of creating a sound infrastructure with intensive internal circulation of goods, the economy and the farmer's well-being itself becomes vulnerable. World market prices are fixed neither in the country nor in the region, but for example, on the commodity markets of Chicago (for corn), of New York (for coffee, sugar), of London (for cacao). It is also a blunder to mitigate the consequences by regularly providing international food aid from stockpiled foods because this action disturbs the internal market, ruins the sound price system as a production incentive and thus further destroys the country's fragile agricultural sector.

Besides producing crops for export, the most important task is to invest in cooperatives which would assure a progressive home-grown development of farming.[3] Of course, these investments must be completed by investment in cottage industry as complementary activity, and by investments for stockpiling grain and food reserves on the local and regional levels.

An appropriate investment policy and reorganization of the agricultural sector supplying the internal market would better the rhythm of the rural-urban migration process without stopping it. Indeed, the pace and direction of rural-urban migration (market-town versus metropolis) should be redressed and not halted. Knowing the strong positive correlation between the urbanization indicator and the population employed in the non-agricultural sector, one should keep in mind that no country with a *GNP* per capita over $1000 has more than 20% of its labor force employed in the agricultural sector, and all large countries of Tropical Africa have more than 50% of their population employed in agriculture (ranging from 83% to 54%; *World Development...*: 170-1). The next step in the development of tropical agriculture should not be extensive one (increased acreage) but an intensive one.[3]

UNDEREMPLOYMENT AND THE RESIDUAL SECTOR

In a transitional society with a dual economy, the number of active persons receiving cash payments for their services increases, while a new category of able-bodied people appears — the so-called unemployed. Cash payment is received as salary or as the price given for produced merchandise. It means purchasing power but also provides the possibility of choice, a means of emancipation. When the household is no longer a productive unit, its members are composed of wage earners and non-earning members. Non-earning members either depend upon public assistance or upon the income distribution effectuated by the household's authority which could be the *paterfamilias*, the wage earner or the household as a collective decision maker.

In a transitional society the number of salaried workers increases but also a relatively large grey zone (or black market of labor forces) appears where officially unemployed people work casually. This zone is very important not only for the casual earners but for the economy itself because it is complementary to the formal sector and fills gaps usefully. It is very difficult to delineate this sector or to take a census of the people working there. Fapohunda (p. 41) estimates that more than 50% of Lagos' metropolitan labor force work in the informal sector, and Aryee evaluates it at 66% for Kumasi in Ghana, while Joshi (p. 106) puts it at 30% for Abidjan and at over 50% for Bouaké (also in the Ivory Coast). The denomination itself varies according to different authors. Most call it the informal sector (Herbert; Jules; Joshi: 49; Gerry about Small-scale Manufacturing and Repairs in Dakar, in Bromley and Gerry), others (B. R. Roberts) call it marginal, which implies a negative connotation and causes opposition by others (such as J. E. Perlman in his study about urban poverty in Rio de Janeiro). The term quarternary sector (Friedman) implies on the contrary, an omnipresent phenomenon which would be in expansion worldwide in both developing and developed (Eastern and Western) economies.

Without doubt, this non-formal sector is defined chiefly by exclusion from the officially recognized formal sector. It may be a subsidiary, but essentially it is a residue; therefore, we call it a residual sector (Ankerl 1984: 43). How can we circumscribe this sector? For the underprivileged urban immigrant the most important characteristic is the fact that it is easy to enter (ILO 1972) the residual sector, in many respects: it is outside the scope of the laws and regulations governing such matters as establishment of shops, workshops, labor permits, labor-management relations, taxation and supervision of technical skill and product quality (Joshi: 49s). Thus "undocumented people", aliens without working permits and diplomas, have easy casual access as a first source of livelihood. Workers in the residual sector rarely have more than a primary education, and some workers are not truly literate. The skills used are mainly acquired outside the formal system of education and training by apprenticeship. The entrepreneur himself sometimes does not have enough numeracy for bookkeeping. Thus the entrepreneur deliberately keeps his business small in order to maintain it under his personal supervision. These small businesses operate on an unregulated (competitive) market, without looking for additonal clients. While they use local resources, rudimentary equipment and flexible labor-intensive technology, each firm rarely has more than two employees in addition to the family members. Since they operate outside of the national taxation and accounting system, they have low "overheads", but they must function without the credit facilities which are at the large firms' disposal. The residual sector is not dynamic, but it is a mushrooming phenomenon. (M. Granovetter: "Small is bountiful.") To assess the significance of the residual sector in terms of job opportunity for the urban underprivileged and as a complement to the national economy, the following basic considerations can be made:

– For the underprivileged, the alternatives to the low income received from the residual sector are either subsistence-farming with its low productivity, or the status of complete unemployment. Even though the residual sector gives barely enough income for the wage earner to sustain himself, and none to keep a family, the role of this sector can be considered in a dynamic way as an apprenticeship where uneducated, unskilled labor learns basic know-how (journeyman first, master craftsman later).

– The volatile nature of the sreidual sector makes it difficult for the authority to help by such means as tax credits. Because of its socioeconomic function, it is certainly not reasonable to reduce this sector by harassment (Fapohunda, Joshi). A tolerant policy which tries to orient this sector in a desirable direction is appropriate. Indeed, not all parts of this sector equally fill their roles as complements to the large formal industry and as places of apprenticeship for uneducated workers. It must be distinguished between cottage indutsry, repair and similar craftsmanship function and criminal activities (drug smuggling, child prostitution; Descloitres in *Croissance:* 543). In order to devise an appropriate policy, not only fine distinctions must be made, but the modality of intervention must be carefully designed.

ELDERLY, HANDICAPPED AND CHILDREN

As we already noted, because of the social transformation involved in urbanization, the handicapped, elderly and children as non-active members of households receive very different treatment in the traditional rural community and in the metropolitan society. The elderly lose their prestigious status which they enjoyed because of their seniority (the experienced wise man; Paulme) in the lineal *gerontocracy*. In absence of subsidiary measures from the government or local authority, they are often in a worsening situatiton because of the disaggregation of the extended family, the existence of single man households and the lack of pension plans in the residual sector.

In the urbanizing Tropical Africa, it is probably the handicapped and chronically ill persons who are in the worst situation. They have no "past services" on their credit as an asset. Many have been left behind by the busy adult migrant in the rural area, and are outside the view of any authority. If they are in the city of a poor country without governmental assistance or help from social organizations, they are street beggars or they rummage through the garbage, or, if they still have access to the common pot, they are the last served when there are any remains.

The child's situation is a crucial issue for the development of a country because the fate of a whole chain of future generations is affected. Concerning their number, recent studies in Kenya (which has the highest population growth rate among the 5 largest countries of Tropical Africa), show that women who live in cities refuse polygamy and have more schooling than women in rural areas, and yet do not have lower fertility than their rural peers.

Concerning child care, vital statistics about infant mortality (table 9) and child death rate (table 10) are the indicators. Unfortunately, we do not have statistics disaggregated according to urban and rural areas. However, we can conclude that Zaire, the least developed populous country (*GDP* per capita) with the highest urbanization indicator and the speediest urbanization process has both the worst child death rate results as well as the slowest improvement (table 10). About infant mortality we have only some statistics from 1975 (table 9) and therefore cannot make conclusions about improvement (except for Kenya). Variation among the countries is small, with Zaire again on the low end.

The importance of child death rate for life expectancy becomes clear by the inverse rank order of the 5 countries according to these two criteria (tables 9 and 10).

In order to improve the situation, undernourishment, lack of infant care and unwholesome child labor must be overcome. Programs which handle the whole context, such as *WIC* seem to be the most efficient. *WIC* is an abbreviation for *Women, Infant and Children*. The program provides special food and health care for nursing mothers and their babies. This program is again more efficient in urban areas.

TABLE 10.

Child death rate

Country	Child death rate (aged 1–4) (per thousand)		
	1960	1979	Decrease between 1960 and 1979
Zaire	36	25	11
Ghana	36	22	14
Nigeria	36	22	14
Tanazania	32	18	14
Kenya	34	15	14

Source: *World Development Report 1981:* 174—5.

WOMEN

Women are often called a minority, which means they are subject to negative discrimination. Women's disadvantages in traditional village and in modern metropoles can be considered both within the household, and if she makes it to the labor market, in her situation as a wage earner.

Ethnographic studies supply us with abundant materials about women's status in the tribe according to its patrilineal or matrilineal clans and patriarchal or matriarchal family organization. Each one involves an intergenerational role division and a division of work which corresponds to education and influence in political decision making.

In African history, we find women in leading roles as well as in economic activities which go well beyond their physical force but in which they are held in very low esteem. Ruler from North Africa, Cleopatre VII (69–30 B. C.) and Lalla Khentha, queen of Morocco (about 1000) are well known (Julien: 127–54, 169–198) but according to Torday, there were also powerful women in Tropical Africa. In Congo, for example, in the Bakuba or Bushongo ethnic group, in the government of King Nyimi there were always two women — his sisters or daughters as guardians of the peace (Paulme: 97). The status of the common woman in the traditional African society is largely related to her role in the division of work. In societies where several types of economic activities coexist, the social esteem and social status follows this descending order: warrior, hunter, herdsman, livestock farmer of large animals, then of smaller ones (poultry, etc.) and finally the cultivator. (The tradition of a "pedestrian civilization" without horse and wheels.) This is true within the extended family and among coexisting ethnic groups (e.g., in Burundi the governing minority is the Tutsi — called also Watutsi or Batutsi — who have a warrior and herdsman tradition and not the Bahutu (or Hutu) of Bantu origin who are cultivators). If the family is agrarian, it is the women who do the hard work (Boserup), as they did in the plant-gathering society where the man was the hunter. After the man claims land for cultivation, the women and children cultivate it and only the sowing and harvesting are common tasks for both sexes. The women also take care of the small domestic animals (poultry) and do some of the artisanal work (basketmaking and pottery), leaving the more prestigious woodworking to men. (The master blacksmith has a special feared and magical status.)

In austral Africa, in the Zambezi region, where agriculture is predominant, women have higher social status and are more influencial than elsewhere. (For the negro-peuls such as Fouta-Toro, Fouta-Djalon, Sokoto and Adamawa, the cultivation of lands is a humiliating occupancy.) Puberty ceremonies and initiation rites also reveal the status according to each sex. (According to Paige, and Paige the "reproductive ritual" is articulated around the main events of the female life-cyle: protecting virginity as a marriage value (menarche), assuring legitimate paternity for the offspring, monitoring the fertile women's activities and the wife's continuous fertility.) In Sudan, where nomadic rearing of the stock is practiced and not agriculture, the initiation of both sexes is a relentless exercise (circumcision and infibulation). In the agricultural region of austral Africa, the initiation is more "peaceful". Among the Nyanja near the lake Malawi, the girl's initiation is more important than the boy's and the girls enjoy a broad sexual liberty as s the case with the Touareg in the Sahara region. The Islam influence among the Berbers of North Africa produced self-effacement of women obliterating them from public life.

It is not Ilsa Glazer-Schuster's novel about *New Women of Lusaka* (NY, 1979) which can convince us that females do not have special incentives to migrate into cities (Joshi: 33–4; Little 1974: 106). In reality, cities allow more autonomy, and repression there is necessarily less intrusive than it can be in rural areas. Many women leave the rural areas following their husbands sometimes to divorce them later, or alone — to free themselves from the constraints of the traditional life-style.

On the road to "social liberation" by rural-urban migration, the remnants of male prejudice and women's lower education are the main reasons for their ultimate deception. In Kenya, for example, male illiteracy is 40% compared to 65% for women (1982).

Contrasting women's participation in the labor market and in so-called professional activities to an intensive and even predominant role in domestic affairs (education, household budget, etc.) is not necessarily a measure of a female's well-being. There are genetic differences between men and women and there is no reason to suppress role divisons in so far as they are truly based on this difference. There is no other reason for a *gleichschaltung* than doctrinaire obstinacy. In the fight against women's unfair treatment two principles must give guidance:

– all differences which are not based on women's different biological constitution and different biological roles (reproduction) must be abolished;

– if for any reason, women (single, for example) are active in the professional life, all job markets must be open to them and they must receive equal reward for equal service.

In reality, females benefit from discrimination by nature in respect to their infant mortality and life expectancy in contrast, for example, to their performance in sports. Using the 1960's data which are at our disposal (*International Populations Office,* US Bureau of the Census; *US World Population Prospects as Assessed in 1973,* Population Studies no. 60, New York City, 1977) we can conclude that in the 20 African countries considered, in no country do women have a lower life expectancy at age one than men, but plotted against other countries the female-male difference varies very strongly: it is 18 years in Gabon but only 0.6 years in Liberia. After a check of the reality of the data, it would be interesting to look for correlation between these data and patri- or matrilineal social systems. In this respect, it is an interesting fact that only in Asia are there countries where women's life expectancy is lower than men's. Going from South to North, the difference in Sri Lanka was 1.8 years (1963), in India 1.0 (1970) and in Afganistan 0.7 (Morris: 153–9). Generally speaking, the difference in male and female life expectancies at age one and the difference in male and female infant mortality is highly correlated. This correlation allows us to theorize about discrimination as a systematic social cause. (In fact, in the 1960's in Liberia, the proportion of female-male infant mortality was 183:160, while the female-male life expectancy difference 0.6 years; the same in 1965 for Cameroon was 130:122 and 1.0 years. We find a similar correlation in India which has a negative female-male life expectancy difference, and the proportion of female-male infant mortality was 138:131 in 1970). If the female's natural advantage in life expectancy at age one disappears in a country in correlation with the higher female infant mortality, this fact can be attributed to negative discrimination in care for female children; but if this correlation is inexistant, man's lower life expectancy can be related to specific death causes which can result from man's more demanding professional and social role. Even from the strictest feminist viewpoint, in the assessment of women's situation, it must always be considered in the framework of the system of social roles as a whole with their feedback and compensatory processes. To be sure, it is easier to posit this requirement than to carry it out in quantitative terms. Concerning the feminization of various occupations, there is a so-called U-shaped hypothesis: after a household income increase women leave the labor force and return to household occupations. We have too few data to contribute to the verification of this hypothesis in Tropical Africa. *UN Patterns...* (p. 91) considers only 10 African countries and 7 are in North Africa. (In Rihani's annotated bibliography *Development as Women Matter* we find sources for further studies.)

Women's move to the cities can have various motives. Between the age of 20 and 40, the search of a male partner is one of them. Joshi (p. 34) and E. Skinner (in Kuper) relate that for example. Mossi women migrate from the North of the Ivory Coast (and even from Upper Volta) to Abidjan because they are outnumbered by the male Mossis, and thus improve their chances for an endogamic marriage as well as their treatment as married women. It is a statistical fact that between 1965 and 1975 males are largely overrepresented in the age group over 20 in African cities, which is not the case for rural areas for the age group 20–40, and in Europe and America in general (*UN Patterns...*: 108, fig. XIII, XIV, XV).

In a broader sense, city life opens the door for underprivileged women to greater freedom of collective and bilateral association, freer choice for casual dating, friends and life partners from other ethnic groups than hers. Voluntary associations of underprivileged in Leopoldville/Kinshasa are also important for mutual aid or just the pleasure of togetherness. How do women make use of such a possibility? Comhaire-Sylvain reports about the Moziki, a women's association in Kinshasa which encourages mutual friendship and organizes the entertainment of independent women (e.g. Saturday night). Curiously women's associations often have men presidents. Bernard (p. 577) notes that while men's associations are often inter-ethnic, married women associate more in mono-ethnic neighborhoods (e.g., immigrants from Angola or from Senegal in Kinshasa). Often this implies that the married women confine themselves to a single section of the city.

NOTES

1. The anthropologist Little (1965: 4-5) wrote:
"Illiterate person: one... who cannot understand or make himself understood in English or French." ."Literate person: ...it excludes... a person who is literate only in Arabic." Scibner and Cole's study about literacy in Vai script, Arabic and English language (made in Liberia) is not exempt from anti-Arabic bias by stating that literacy in Arabic is irrelevant for modernization. But this study also shows that literacy is less relevant for socialization in a modern society than schooling where appropriate cognitive skills are learned.

2. Gugler found (Gilber: 53) similar urban superiority concerning infant mortality (in %) in the Central African Republic (1960) 12%, Gabon (1960) 71%, Kenya (1977) 21%, Senegal (1973) 93%, Tanzania (1973) 38% and in Togo (1961) 26%.

3. Cooperatives allow the introduction of new agrotechniques. Sanchez and Buol state (p. 603):
"While basic concepts about physical and chemical behavior developed in the nonglaciated temperate regions are directly applicable to the tropics, the development of soil management practices for sustained food production involves different strategies because of environmental and economic constraints. A major distinction is made between the development of high base status and low base status soils. [The latter] are in the vast savanna and jungle areas where crop varieties and species more tolerant to nutritional deficiencies or toxicities [must be chosen] and fertilizers at lower rates must be applied."

CHAPTER THREE

THE SEARCH FOR SOLUTIONS

RURAL-URBAN MIGRATION: POLICY GOALS AND MEASURES FOR DECELERATION AND REDIRECTION

We took stock of the urbanization process in the 5 largest countries of Tropical Africa mainly in quantitative terms and assessed the manner in which this process affects the fate of the underprivileged stratum of the population. Some central problems emerge which must be solved in priority. One is that of urban congestion which can be prevented by slowing and redirecting migration. The present level of the urbanization indicator in Tropical Africa is low compared to the world average as well as in relation to the prospect of economic transformation which would diminish the agrarian population and improve the overall efficiency of the national economy; therefore, a future increase of the urban indicator should be anticipated. However, as we have seen before, in terms of already accomplished structural (economic) transition and economic development measured in *GDP* per capita, the present level of urbanization no longer seems to be low, especially in Zaire, the poorest of the 5 countries. We also see that Zaire leads in the rapid increase of its urbanization indicator (table 7; *Croissance:* 26–7, 41). When we consider urban concentration, we see (tables 5 and 6) that it increases in all 5 populous countries despite the rapid development of non-primate cities such as Kananga in Zaire. (The federal structure of Nigeria and the construction of the new federal capital, the centrally located Abuja which is at the confluence of Hausa, Yoruba and Ibo ethnic groups will somewhat deflate Lagos' primacy.) Even if the rapid development of the non-agricultural sector could fully employ the rural migrants, (which is not the case,) public services cannot keep pace with the rapid urbanization without degrading urban life, and the private sector cannot respond to the demand of goods and services without soaring prices, especially in housing.

As we have seen, the increase of the urbanization indicator and of the concentration indexes comes mainly from rural migration; therefore, it is a reasonable policy goal to slow down and redirect this latter. We must now look more closely at the specific causes accelerating rural-urban migration in black Africa and also at those factors which could be influenced by policy in the most convenient manner.

Special attention must be attached to the redirection of the migration from the metropolis to other urban areas.

Beyond the simple preference for decentralization, countries of Tropical Africa have two main reasons to insist on the development of cities other than the metropolis:

1. Among the 37 primate cities, 28 are peripherally situated in respect to their countries and 22 are ports (Clarke in *Croissance*: 448-9). They are either seaports with orientation to the world market, or river ports which convey raw materials to the colonial metropoles. These cosmopolitan cities often have only peripheral African sections constructed originally for transient sojourn (e.g. Treichville in Abidjan, Bernard: 576-7, about Leopoldville/Kinshasa). Still, especially large countries need a network of cities, and development of cities with central locations in relation to the national territory ("heartland"). This autonomous infrastructure woulds promote the country's internal communication and market.

2. Some smaller cities in the hinterland have better preserved their African character than the cosmopolitan capitals. (This is especially the case in the French colonies where Colberism promoted a strong centralization. See Abidjan in relation to Bouaké in the Ivory Coast. Chevassu: 433s; Clarke in *Croissance*: 450; Joshi: 96.) It is time to revive the tradition of the African market town (this urban tradition in Africa has often been ignored by the rural oriented anthropologists) instead of promoting carbon copies of the Euro-American metropolis such as Plateau in downtown Abidjan as a Little Manhattan of New York City. Fassassi gives many examples of urban African tradition.[1]

These cities which are often more centrally located but which are secondary in importance today have not only remained more African than the cosmopolitan capitals but also have preserved the daily contact with their immediate rural environment (market), and for these reasons allow a much better integration of the immigrant population. They offer a better apprenticeship for urban living with fewer ruptures, — an especially important aspect in the case of rapid urbanization where the first generation urban residents are numerous (*UN Patterns*: 101E.).

Let us now see the causes of rural-urban migration and the factors which can restrain it. As in any research, two approaches are possible: an objective one which looks for strong correlation between migration and other (behavioral) processes, and a subjective one which scrutinizes the incentives for migration in the migrant's decision-making.

Based on the World Bank's *World Tables* (1971, 1976), the UN team calculated (*UN Patterns*: 31-3) the zero-order correlation coefficients between rural net out-migration rate and some demographic and economic indicators for 29 developing countries in the Third World. We can

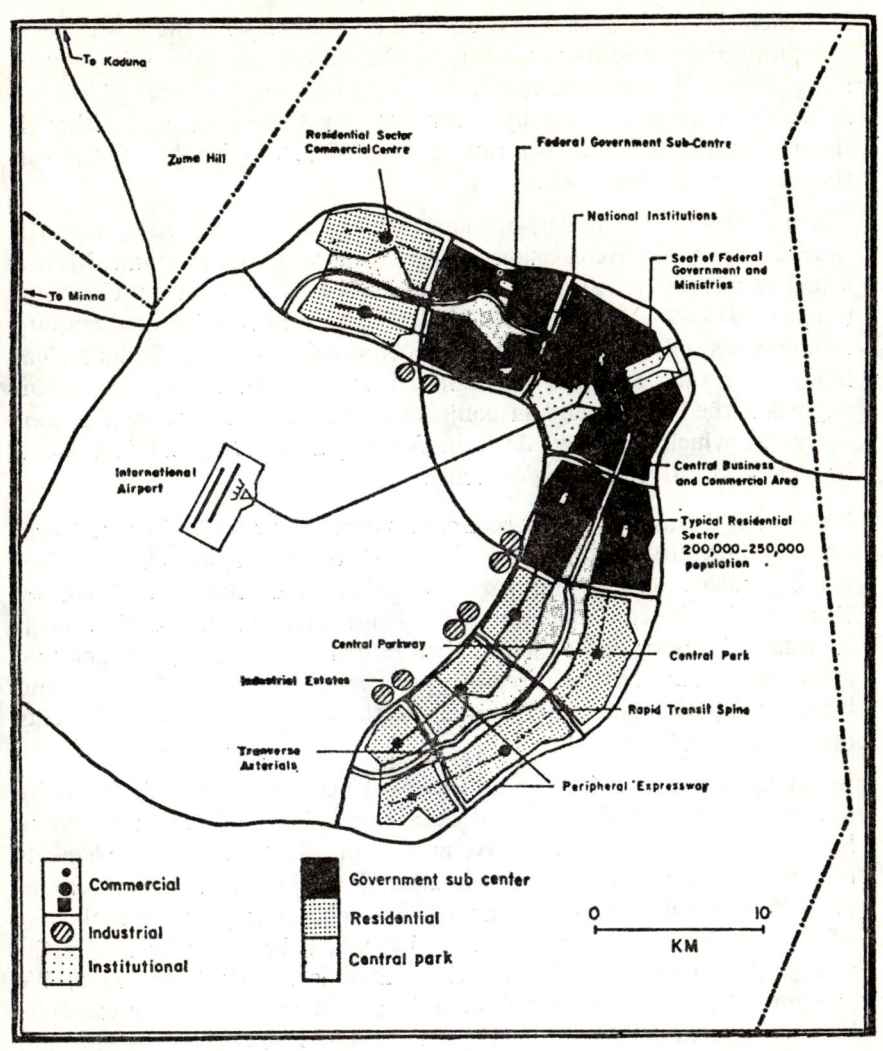

Abuja: city plan adopted in 1979

state that rural net out-migration has a positive correlation to the initial *GNP* per capita (0.611), to the absolute growth rate in *GDP* per capita (0.548), and to the initial urbanization indicator (0.576). The rural net out-migration is not negatively correlated to the growth rate of agricultural production per rural resident (+0.466) (i.e., to the increase in agricultural productivity). The comparison of these correlations shows that the initial income level seems to be a better predictor of the rural-urban migration process than the initial level of the urbanization indicator.

However, this initial level has a positive correlation with the process as if the rural-urban migration were a cumulative and partially self-perpetuating process. We must consider these results with caution because Tropical Africa is represented only by Ghana among these countries, although the UN research team does not find significant regional variations in these correlation coefficients.

There are numerous models of migration behavior explained by the attitude, i.e. the subjective decision-making of the would-be migrants. Motive is a treacherous territory for the researcher as we exposed elsewhere (Ankerl 1973, 1981). Motives are hidden from even sophisticated enquiry by numerous veils; motives may be unacknowledged even by the individual himself, or they may not be admitted to the interviewer, etc. Urban migration theories abound in conjectures, but there is not even a consensus at which level the decision for migration is made: individual, household or other sociological units.

Neo-classical and marginalist economists developed spatial theories based on very unrealistic assumptions. These theorists imagine illiterate man making calculations of his expected urban-rural income differentials. These models based on the *homo economicus* remain unrealistic even if they have been refined (Todero, then Harris and Todero) by replacing actual differences by the perceived prospect of income differential, and by enlarging the salary differential by the concept of overall benefits (including social services).

In reality, those who (a) can and (b) will make calculated decisions by using modern game theories and decision-making models (Morgenstern, Neuman and Harsanyi) do not live in African villages. In fact, the elements of this calculation are not even available. Who knows the coefficient of probability (c) which describes the migrant's chance to get a job in the city which provides a higher income than that which he presently has in the village? (The rural-urban income differential is not contested here. We recognize that this differential even increased in Nigeria, for example, between 1960 and 1977 from 1:2.6 to 1:4.6. *World Development*: 90; Ginneken.) The broadening of the concept of expected income differential to the overall benefit (Harris and Todero) adds a new disadvantage to the model because in this case the model cannot be numerically effectuated (d).

Economists' rationalistic models are based on amateur sociopsychologicial assumptions. Lewis and Fei–Ranis theorize in the spirit of optimistic functionalism where the rural-urban migration is simply a rational deployment of the surplus agricultural manpower into the industrial sector in order to find new equilibrium at a higher level of efficiency for the national economy.

Generally speaking, motives of migration can be as various as motives of human behavior. From an ecological viewpoint, a living being can respond to unsatisfied need in 3 manners:

- transforming the environment (the technological response),
- adapting himself to the need perception by accepting the situation (psychological adjustment), or
- leaving the milieu by migration.

Before we can study the disincentives a government can apply, we should add some specifications for "migration". We understand here rural-urban migration, i.e. a more or less permanent change of residence from an area which has less "extensive density" to one which has more. (Relevant magnitudes are defined by the country's local census authority. *UN Patterns...*: 121-4) This definition of migration implies some degree of sedentariness. On the other hand, if somebody changes his working place from a rural to an urban area, it is not migration if he commutes daily between his initial residence and his new working place (which is possible in case of adequate transportation facilities). By contrast, residential change is an overall decision. It involves numerous characteristics of the initial locality and those of the locality of destination with all their attractive and unattractive aspects. All these are in relation to the decision-making units which could be either a clan, a peer group, a household or a single individual, each with its own characteristics (biological, psychological, professional and educational) (Ankerl 1974: 577, 580-4). Finally, the distance of the migration with its possible obstacles is the spatial aspect (Lee, Amin). The authority can play upon these aspects as disincentives to migrate in their relation to the symptoms indicating the most important reasons for migration in a specific situation.

DISINCENTIVES TO MIGRATION

In general we can put the attractive and unattractive aspects of rural and urban life into 3 groups: productive, consumptive and social.

1. As we are concerned here especially with households without independent means, employment as the sole source of income is an important factor. For the worker, the elements of comparisons are the monetary part of income, the in kind, insurance and other social benefits, and, on the other side, the type and duration of the work. However, the balance cannot be done on a global basis: in the village the non-cash component of the input side can be higher for a household than in the cities; but

this non-cash allotment excludes full consumer freedom which has a value of its own (Ankerl 1978: 65). On the productive front, the disincentive for migration is creation of employment in the original locality mainly by investment and the dissemination of this fact by the mass media: radio, TV. Of course, investment policy must be guided at first by its short-, middle- and long-term profitability — the latter is difficult to calculate with accuracy and is rarely done; therefore, no government should encourage investment in the locality far from raw materials and far from a market with poor transportation just for the sake of local employment. Yet, the relatively cheaper manpower can be an incentive on its own. From the viewpoint of the national economy, if the rural-urban migration brings an important diminution in the agricultural output, it is an indication that the authority should make more investments in rural development. (Of course, few countries can afford to diminish their agricultural production.)

2. With the exception of self-fulfilling work, the productive side of life is basically an instrument for consumption, which provides enjoyment. The consumption side is already tangled with the income side because the purchasing power depends upon the price level. Therefore, price policy can be used as a disincentive for migration. In reality, until the distribution system (middleman system) creates higher prices for local (e.g., agricultural) products in small town markets than in the metropoles, the government can also influence migration by price policy through the regulation of large monopolistic distributions. The attractiveness of the consumption side of the city is the larger choice of merchandise; new products are often available in the metropolis and not at all elsewhere.

3. The attraction of urban life encompasses a whole "syndrome". In reality, in so far as we can distinguish the urban from the rural, in cities we find more specialized products, services and entertainment of quality offered in an economical manner. These cultural amenities predominate over the natural ones. Africans often practice a very intensive life-style (Little). For this reason, the bright lights of the cities which make possible an active life around the clock (e.g. Treichville in Abidjan) are very important. According to Bernard, Kinshasa's center received more public lighting after independence than before; see also the search for light effects in Yamoussoukro, the new capital of the Ivory Coast.

On the other hand, the urban life also includes a different social network (Ankerl 1974: 580 fig. 5; 1981). People who like to frequently see varied people, to have a large choice to meet and to communicate with people to whom they have no genealogical kin or socially well-defined formal relations, like to move to the city for this social variety and independence.

Rural and urban life-style is a choice. This choice is, of course, made by young individuals who often carry along their "brothers and sister" (and brothers of brothers), maybe the whole household or even the compound. And in the clan exogamy these tribal networks constitute a quasi-infinite web (Decloîtres and Boutillier in *Croissance*: 371-4, 526).

In order to apply an efficient disincentive to urban in-migration the first step, on the objective level, is the careful analysis of the situation in the metropolis and rural areas. Which is more critical in the metropolis — unemployment or the housing situation? If the difficulty is on the supply side (e.g. housing), this means that the better employment situation (in terms of offer and income) in the city is an important incentive for migration, and therefore, additional job opportunities offered elsewhere can slow down metropolitan in-migration, or redirect it. Yet, on the objective level, other aspects can be comparatively evaluated and the best disincentive inferred. In fact, even if the rural-urban migration stream is high in the whole of Tropical Africa, its main causes and directions are not uniform.

After the assessment of the objective situation, on the subjective side better information must correct distortion of the metropole's image. This is a delicate task. Usually television and all central media broadcast from the metropolises and the government which tries to create a national identity and unity beyond ethnic diversity has the interest to promote national symbols, the image of the capital being one of them. This cannot be done by objective reporting. (Even overdeveloped countries like Switzerland take care of the image of their cities: television reporters are penalized for publicizing Zurich as an unsafe city because the number of people arrested in 1981 for revolt was as high as 1% of the population.) However, more objective information about the living conditions of all social strata in the metropolis is an efficient way to discourage further immigrants. Certainly, media cannot solve the whole problem of misinformation because even unsuccessful urban immigrants continue to entertain a mythical image of the metropolitan life in order to protect their own prestige in the native village. Considering the complexity of the problem, it is not an unwise solution for the government to develop cities as showcases in the central area of the country. This would be a symbol of newly obtained independence, a symbol of a new nation, and at the same time it would make a sounder network of the country's cities. This would also discourage remigration from the centrally located cities to the old coastal metropolises, especially if various cities had different functions (administrative, commercial, etc.). Properly distributed city networks would create a better infrastructure. In this way, a household might opt for a mixed life-style where some members commute, perhaps on a seasonal basis, and others continue to farm in the countryside. But for this restructuring, using already existing cities would be more appropriate than the very expensive founding of brand new cities. (Development of Buoaké in the Ivory Coast instead of Yamoussoukro.)

A final entangling problem should not be neglected: housing and unemployment problems are already existent in all large cities. When the authority focuses on their solution, new difficulties arise. In reality, in-migration will accelerate and a true vicious circle is created. For this very reason, it is detrimental to chiefly concentrate on solving problems in the metropolis just because it is an international and national showcase and because the danger of social eruption is higher. Budgetary allocation should be evenhandedly distributed among the various cities, according to cost-benefit analyses. Strictly applied, this requirement would exclude rural areas from some allocations because their cost-effectiveness is worse. However, as the overall social costs of disfunctional migration are very high, some public investment in rural areas is advisable, even if in a short-term calculation it seems to be less economical than the same expenditure in urban areas. Measures of public assistance and improvement of public services are especially important in case of famine, disaster, etc. when the tendency to migrate is obviously strong.

SOCIAL PROBLEM-SOLVING BY COLLECTIVE SELF-HELP

As we have just seen, many studies in Tropical Africa show that ethnic and relational ties are important elements for the assessment of the flow of migration. We can now ask the question — how deeply (in intensity and duration) do these ties continue to assure the function of a solidarity network for the resourceless unemployed, disabled, children and elderly? To what extent have these ties been shrunk — from ethic group to extended family, from compound to household — and to what point will they be succeeded by more modern forms of association (voluntary associations, peer groups, etc.)? How well do these new social networks fulfill the tasks of social problem-solving for all groups of the society (new types of solidarity contracts of Albert Tévoédjrè)? Is more governmental intervention needed (Ankerl 1978: 26; 1980: 7–10)? Whether collective self-help or the government solves social problems makes a difference in their outcome. In all likelihood, in the case of sustained governmental intervention by social policy, the beneficiary becomes a passive recipient. Furthermore, the remote public bureaucracy as an all-provider often misreads the genuine needs and distributes its in kind allowance which easily leads to waste.

In the solution of social problems, participation is often evoked. It means voluntary sharing on the part of the beneficiary but does not necessarily require his initiative. (If we demand the individual's initiative, we should bear in mind that the idea itself comes from the individualistic and actualistic philosphy of Western civilization.) There are many reasons to give preference to all kinds of self-help. It activizes the person himself and mobilizes his capacities. This measure would be immediate in its effect and appropriate in its manner because the recipient directly perceives what he wants. (This is preferable even at the risk that he make mistakes in the perception of his long-term needs if he does not seek advice.) However, self-help can be efficient in so far as the person concerned has sufficient means at his disposal and the assisted persons are usually short of means. Therefore, a second step in self-help is to encourage spontaneous association of these persons and others for collective self-help (Cohen: 215–6). As we already mentioned, a social system finds its optimal functioning when the principle of subsidiarity is respected: all problems are to be solved at the lowest possible institutional level and only when means at the lower level have been exhausted must the problem be referred to a higher one (Ankerl 1965: 144 fig.; 1978: 73–74).

In the concrete situation of Tropical Africa today, we should consider that small is not beautiful per se (Schumacher) and that in an urbanized modern society many tasks of income distribution and equalization cannot be solved on a narrow local level; on the other hand, for a strategy to organize collective self-help, it is necessary to know which existing and emerging solidarity ties are actually present in a transitional society and which have become antiquated. Before solidarity ties can be assessed, social networks should be studied (Mitchell, Warren).

SOCIAL NETWORKS

The traditional social network was a relatively closed one for tribes whether sedentary or nomadic. Except for relations with foreign merchants, nearly all human relationships were based on mutual intergenerational knowledge. (Bamilekes, for example, trace their lineal genealogy back to 4 generations, Yorubas to 10.) Tribal endogamy worked to unite and close up relations between the clans lodged on their compounds. Tribal order had been enhanced in most of the cases by the lingual and ethnic community. Rural-urban migration with its internal and often international nature transforms the stable pattern of the primary group. The various phases of migration — first arrival, followed by kin, and then the next generation born in the city — modifies the "size" of the We-group, viz., the in-group feeling: the clan's solidarity has shrunk to the lineal family's, even if here and there the necessities of international migration occassionally heightened the clan's solidarity to an ethnic or tribal one (chieftainship transplanted in urban areas; Zabramas' super-tribalism following migration from Niger to Ghana (Little 1965: 24, 47) or solidarity among immigrant Mossis in the Ivory Coast coming from Burkina Faso.) On the other side, the widening of the elective relationship beyond ethnic bonds dilutes the clan's unity (tribal exogamy, interethnic marriages and even interethnic peer groups) and introduces individuals in the primary solidarity network whose family "heritage" is rarely known. These introduced fortuitous factors make relations more ephemeral.

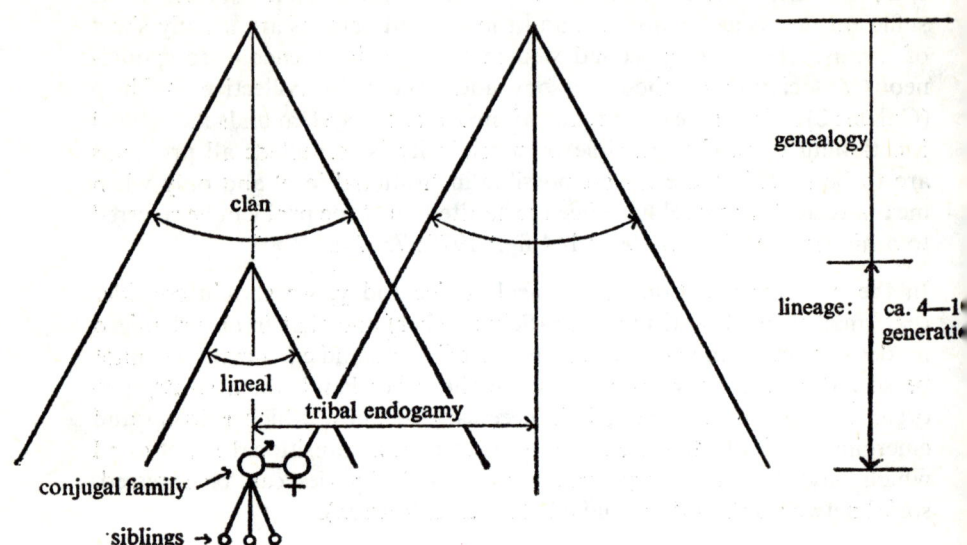

Kinship: Consanguineal and affinal relationships.

In the multifaceted transformation of the mainly rural-based society into the urbanized and non-agricultural one (of course, neither pastoral nor hunting), we should sort out characteristics which are primarily relevant for mapping the social networks which will show persistent solidarity links in urban Africa.

The urbanization process as transition implies at least two typical tendencies:

1. The separation of the household and the productive unit takes place even if the cottage industry and other small businesses remain family based. (In the old ecologically rooted unit, age, sex and genealogy were the basic differentiators for social organization. (Paulme: 74–5, 87, 103.)

2. Mobility becomes a personal affair. People move spatially. They change residence individually or in other formations than the extended family. This type of moving is not simply in the tradition of neolocal residence. Siblings, ethnic peer groups, family fractions or other local groups move. They marry outside the original tribe, and the old kinship unit is never again recovered, even if this broader trend is accompanied by paradoxal counter-tendencies: first generation urban in-migrants often have larger families and stronger kinship ties than others left behind in the village.

Without making any value judgment by speaking about progress, in the societal planning where we will construct collective self-help organizations which persist through the change, we should look for potential solidarity links in light of these basic aspects of the transition.

Solidarity ties are inconceivable without linkage. We must first learn which social links have subsisted or have been newly woven in the urbanization process accompanied by migration. Since the anthropologist Radcliffe–Brown (in 1952) defined social structure as a network of actually existing social relationships, and A. Bavelas and C. Flament gave a solid methodological underpinning to the social network analysis by application of the graph theory, numerous sample surveys have been carried out in Tropical Africa. (One of the first comprehensive publications handled surveys mainly carried out in Lusanka and elsewhere in the former Northern Rhodesia (now Zambia) by J. C. Mitchell et al.) Recent studies (Holland; White) show many variations in the application of this method from purely metaphorical approaches to analytical ones. Along with other flows and linkages, there is the communication network (or channels) and structure (or flows) which most specifically characterize all social formations (Rogers). Spatial positions, such as encounters and shared dwellings determine the communication network as a possibility of face-to-face (or of indirect) communication (letters, phone calls, smoke signs, drums or whistling as telecommunication). The network itself includes potential communication flows which could be realized as an actual communication structure. As a matter of fact, urbanization fundamentally changes the duration, frequency and number of persons involved in communications as well as the length of their acquaintance — communications which various individuals entertain with their relatives, neighbors and members of their households (Ankerl 1974: 574s; 1981: 67s). The patterns of communication structure which characterize the social formations themselves have changed by the historical transition. The map of communication networks (e.g. living together) and actual communication flows (e.g. daily exchange with kins during a whole lifetime, *UN Patterns*: 96) is a fine barometer for showing actual linkage for possible solidarity ties. Gibbal (p. 388) notes, for example, that second generation in-migrants in Abidjan tend to make more and more seldom the encounter with fellow tribe members who do not belong to the more limited clan or even lineal family; and his readiness to assist extends only to those tribe fellows whom he had known personally before. On the other hand, they extend their communication structure — and solidarity ties — more readily to fellow workers (individuals having the same working place or at least belonging to the same professional association). This and similar hypotheses can be empirically tested by the communication network and structure approach in rural and urban areas of any country using sample survey (maybe investigated previously by case studies).

EFFECTIVE SOLIDARITY TIES

> "In objective terms, solidarity occurs if elements adhere to one and another and show a certain dependence. ... According to this minimal definition:
> – intensity of dependence,
> – duration of it, and
> – the unilateral or multilateral nature of the relationship characterize the solidarity" (Ankerl 1980: 4).

Solidarity given by consanguinity (1) or contracted by choice (2) — by affinity (2a) or simple coalition (2b) — can be measured by its intensity and relative strength.

– The degree of intensity of solidarity is manifested by self-forgetfulness, by being at one with one's partners — in extreme, by an overwhelming We-feeling.

– A further aspect of solidarity is its relative strength. Men with equal readiness to share can concentrate their solidarity on a more or less large circle of people and in case of conflict of loyalty make their choices by establishing a priority order (Ankerl 1980: 5–11).

Historical transition as the urbanization process changes the communication network and the terms of solidarity contracts (Tévoédjrè). As we discussed, in the traditional African community the extended family commanded a complete organization where hierarchical and successional orders were well established. Children, the sick and the elderly were assisted in principle in this framework and according to the community's philosophy (e.g. Bantu) and to their limited means. The limited means of the family were eventually completed by the tribe which assured some redistributive functions for the benefit of the impoverished compounds (Blanc and Descloîtres in *Croissance*: 37 and 526).

In a mobile urban society it is impossible for the inmigrant to completely recreate this network with its precise solidarity ties and with all the functions it had in the rural community. In the cities, new so-called voluntary organizations emerge which are specialized and open. Because of the demography of in-migration, the young man becomes the central figure (Bernard: 579) and in many respects his peer group replaces the order of lineal gerontocracy. Characteristics of the solidarity ties themselves change. A very intensive communication structure develops with frequent all-directional exchange. (Lombard calls it a kind of gregarious "societomania"; Gibbal 398.) In this climate more or less ephemeral associations are blossoming. Mercier (p. 397s) estimates that 66% of Dakar's inhabitants are members of a political party and P. Marris notes that 50–60% of Lagos' population belongs to some association or society (Little 1965: 164). As we discussed, the syndrome of the urban communication network and structure in contrast to the rural community is well established in general (Ankerl 1974, 1983a), and in today's Tropical Africa in particular, on a higher level in terms of frequency and numbers of interlocutors, even if further studies are needed especially in Eastern and Middle Africa. The crucial question is: does there result from this new communication network and structure a framework for new solidarity contracts which replace the "traditional African social security system" based on ecologically oriented, intuitive and collectivistic community spirit (Senghor: 36–7)? This new association mentality does create durable webs in terms of contractual solidarity whether it cooperates with surviving lineal, clan or ethnic formations or transforms them? In particular, what is the precise relation between the new peer group associations and the traditional fraternal interest groups (Paige), sibling groups such as practiced in Eastern Africa by Nandi, Masai, Suk (Paulme: 74–75) and also in other regions (Bernard; Little 1974; Descloîtres in *Croissance*: 529, 533)? Further scientific mapping of these social webs especially in terms of the durability of adherence of individuals (taken by social categories: in-migrants, etc.) to specific social formation would be very instructive in order to learn how the gap in solidarity organization between the nuclear family and the national government is and will be solved in urban Africa. We cannot insist enough upon the importance of the development of relatively stable and multiple social formations situated between the family and the government even if the government can and must be considered as the last safeguard, a kind of umbrella to intervene everywhere in the societal field where other organizations have failed. But instead of hastily filling the gap, the government must leave enough room for non-patronized organizations, viz. for the "informal sector of the social policy". One of the dangers is the patronizing of even such social organizations as sportive, musical, ethnic ones by the country's one-party. (Verhaegen; Bernard: 582–3). This means not only authoritarianism but totalitarianism. In many countries this phenomenon has a historical background: the fight for independence made unity a value of paramount importance and encouraged the existence of charismatic historical leaders (the fatherly "old man" modeled on de Gaulle in the former colonies). (In countries where the leader did not have this historical charisma, authoritarianism is seen more critically.)

In all transitional societies, it is especially necessary not only for the average person's social security but even for his mental health to have about 4 persons (Ankerl 1972: 56) with whom he shares time, intensive social relationships and a common personal history creating understanding and a primary solidarity.[2] This comes from the rearing shared on a compound, or in a neighborhood and shared vernicular language. The elite, forgetting their ethnic roots, often replace childhood camerades by alumni associations. Working class individuals usually prefer more ethnic based church organizations (Bernard; Little). (The disintegration of the extended family ties in American cities also increases the homeless street people. *New York Times,* January 29, 1986.)

In order to effectively solve problems of income distribution by redistribution among members, it is necessary to have within the framework of the organization persons who have more than the others. Certain income differences are temporary: a child will earn later, as perhaps the unemployed, and the elderly may have their savings; their problems can be solved by an organization of mutual aid if it has sufficient size, durability and a sound age composition (cf. actuarial mathematics) where a large share belong to the active population. The UN team (*UN Patterns*: 94) states that "in transitional societies, adults often face a double obligation of providing for both parents and children, and the stress associated with such obligations affects all family members". (This obligation is only stressful if it is restrained to the nuclear family.) According to Little (1965: 27) in Accra some associations have as many as 2000 members. There are many friendly societies, mutual benefit organizations, rotating credit associations, clubs such as esusu for the Yoruba, susu in Kumasi (Ghana), adaski for the Hausa in the North of Nigeria, osusu of the Ibo in South-East Nigeria, njonu in Benin, bandoi in Kinshasa, tontines for the Bamilekes (Cameroon), or djana among the Fang in Southern Cameroon. (Little 1965: 51–2 and Meillassoux mentions others for Bamako in Mali.) There is no reason to renounce spontaneous organizations based on home-grown solidarity ties for purely ideological reasons by labeling infallibly some social phenomena as reactionary and other marginal phenomena as "avant-garde". This reasoning is often simply based on doctrinaire and wishful thinking.

Voluntary associations as devices to solve members' social problems can have two different tendencies:

1. Trade union tendency: it recruits homogeneous elements to have a better bargaining power (collective bargaining) and thus to increase the overall share of its members in the gross national product. This does not exclude an additional function, namely, internal redistribution among the members. These organizations are fundamentally interethnic and class-oriented, calling for class solidarity, even if some are articulated along ethnic lines because of the mono-ethnic compositions of some professions (Gibbal: 388; Little 1974: 47, 95). (As a matter of fact, because of the migrant's use of clan connections, some ethnic groups monopolize some sectors where unlearned workers are often absorbed. E.g. petty traders in Ghana are the Zabramas, yam trade in Kumasi is in Gas hands and the richer Ashanti are mainly in the manufacturing industry. (A similar specialization can be observed by the Chinese, Italian, etc. immigrants in the USA.) Though the trade union's solidarity is based on the idea that sophisticated organization strengthens bargaining power, those persons without a skill or trade much in demand cannot really form a trade union.

2. Community tendenacy: this organization is more production oriented and implies complementarity. Here the main base of agreement is not the similarity of the income source nor that of the bargaining position. It can be an *association d'originaire* with shared vernicular language, belonging to an ethnic minority (among other ethnic groups). These organizations have a less egalitarian internal order, where people with very different incomes cooperate in a vertical organizational order (Bernard: 579). They often have a patronizing tendency with tribal notables in the governing body (Hassa). The existing income differences among the members makes it possible to exert an important internal redistributive function, but the possibility of such a strategy for solving social problems is realistic only if the shared values — religious, magic, clan, ethnic — allow the members to develop a strong (We- or) in-group feeling, necessary for this type of solidarity contract. In modern times, most of the cases where people tried to transfigure the agrarian community (for example, on a sectarian basis instead of the traditional kinship basis) to an industrial setting as production unit, the outcome was deceiving, with extreme aberrations and even exploitation (cf. Jonestown).

Non-class oriented nonprofit social organizations can solve social problems on a cooperative basis. However, the gap existing in the social field between the nuclear family and the government should not be filled by profit-making enterprises (as is advocated nowadays by President Reagan).

In reality it is enough that companies compete on the labor market to employ the active population by offering reasonable salaries and humane working conditions while leaving after-hour activities to the worker himself; otherwise, the employer's paternalistic attitude would reduce the worker's privacy, frustrate his emancipation, offend his dignity and hinder his mobility in addition to disturbing the good functioning of the whole competitive economic system (Ankerl 1978: 74).

The most underprivileged in tropical urban Africa are not the proletariate who sell their working capacity to live, but what we call the subproletariate. The subproletarian is not numerate though he must compete in a monetary market and has no salable skills for the formal sector of production. These people do not even have the choice to join a trade union despite their inborn capacities which can be developed at work and despite the fact that they represent very cheap manpower. They often live together as squatters or in slums. There are very few permanent consolidated organizations which undertake the task to make these forces useful in cooperatives. Government and other organizations with means at their disposal should invest in these adventures. (Funds of the Swiss Development Fund for Latin America funneled through the Inter-American Development Bank into the Guyana fishing cooperation show, for example, that truly small sums measured in not more than thousands of dollars often bring trangible progress to cooperatives, associations and individuals.) With small loans, these cooperatives can directly improve their members' living conditions by do-it-yourself work (e.g., bungalow-like wooden houses in Gonzagueville near Abidjan's airport), and can produce goods for local use (selling on the roadside market) or maybe even for larger markets. (Of course, often the major hindrance to improve spontaneous settlements is the unstable legal status of the settlers *(La croissance périphérique)*. Around Abidjan for example, it is possible to evict them at any time because of traditional land possessory rights.

If anywhere, it is especially in a transitional society that solutions, lasting or not, must be found for every day because this diminishes each day's suffering. For this reason all authorities who possess power must act in a continuous way: bridging short-term problem-solving with long-term visions. Assuring day-to-day survival is perhaps a banal task and often the solution is not less banal; it often consists in the recognition of the importance of collective self-help which should be encouraged with limited financial means. Thus all kinds of solidarity ties could be mobilized, either coming from peoples' common past experience, their present situation or their shared aspirations.

NOTES

1. According to William Bascom, (Urbanization among the yoruba, in *American Journal of Sociology*, 1955: 446-54), around 1930-40 in the Yoruba region there were more people (37.4%) living in cities of over 5000 than there were in France (31.7%) (Fassassi: 82). In fact, in Nigeria, Ibadan has old Yoruba traditions, Kano (XV century) has Hausa traditions, and Ile-Ife, Oyo and Ekiti are cities with traditions from the old Benin empire. Kumbi (300-1200) was the capital of the Ghana empire; Mogadishu, Somalia is a historical city as is Mombasa, Kenya and Sofala, ancient Zimbabwe. Sofala, Mogadishu and Mombasa had large regional oriented markets as did Kiloa in Tanzania. In Tropical Africa only the cities founded between 1787 and 1960 are European cities (Fassassi: 21, 97, 99, 121). Gibbal (398) and Little (1974: 99s) found that in contrast to Abidjan, Accra and Lome have a life-style which still shows its African roots. (See also pp. 113—4.)

2. According to *UN Patterns* (p. 98) the average size of a household in rural as well as in urban Benin was in 1961 4.5 persons, in Zimbabwe (Rhodesia in 1962) the urban households had 4 and the rural 5.4 members on the average.

CHAPTER FOUR

SUMMARY OF POLICY RECOMMENDATIONS

1. This study is concerned by the questions: how does the urbanization process as an aspect of transition in *Tropical Africa (T. A.)* affect the underprivileged's situation and how can this situation be improved? Other issues (the social, historical and geographical context of the system) were discussed only if their neglect would have distorted the analysis. For practical reasons we focused our attention on the 5 most populous countries of *T.A.*[1] namely, Nigeria, Zaire, Tanzania, Kenya and Ghana. They contain largely more than half of *T.A.*'s population; also, large countries have different development profiles than small ones (e.g., external vs. internal trade). The denomination Tropical Africa *(T.A.)* also indicates that the tropics constitute a particular setting for some problems and their appropriate solutions in developing countries.

It is proper that recommendations have specifically designated addresees who have the best means to intervene. For this study the addressees are the Organization of African Unity, the regional and subregional organizations (e.g., annual conferences), governments and local authorities. According to the principle of subsidiarity, it is important which level of government addresses a problem, that is to say, not only the efficiency of the intervention but also its outcome may be affected. A particular type of recommendation is not to intervene at all in order to prevent the kind of overgrowth of bureaucracy and counterproductive harassment of spontaneous processes by regulation which is commonly observed in overdeveloped countries *(ODC)*.

For economical reasons, expert reports are based on data already available. Yet, on the other hand, efficiency of action depends largely upon the availability of reliable and relevant up-to-date information; therefore, it is suitable to include suggestions about enlargement of the data base and about further studies in the Recommendations.

1.1. Though Japan and "Western" and "Eastern" (European) countries showed important variations during the last two centuries while on the road to producing "more transformed goods per capita", they *all* underwent a *fundamental urbanization* process.

1.2. While presently *T.A.* is a region of the world where the lowest percentage of the population lives in cities, it is detrimental to accept the anthropologists' bucolic bias which systematically ignores the existence of precolonial urban tradition. Therefore, the appropriate questions are the following:

– Which is the suitable rate of increase of the urbanization indicator in relation to a country's economic indicators (development of production)?

– What are the preferable directions of rural-urban migration?

– What kind of urbanization takes best into account the underprivileged's situation?

2. Urbanization overspeed, and urban concentration:

Urbanization overspeed happens if the rate of urbanization increase is not matched by the level of economic development which determines the means available in a country to bear the overload due to the urbanization process as a structural change. We found that the lower a country's average income level, the higher the urbanization overspeed index (column 6 of table 7); therefore, Zaire is in a critical situation. (The present trend is always represented by the tendency spanning the period 1970–2000.)

Middle Africa is the most and Eastern Africa the least urbanized part of *T.A.* The existing gulf between Middle Africa and rural Eastern Africa will increase until 2000 (even until 2025).

Urban concentration can more or less accompany and aggravate the urbanization process. Various aspects of the network of cities are measured by indexes (tables 4, 5, 6). Kinshasa is *T.A.*'s largest city and remains so through the century while other million-cities[2] of the region including Kananga in Zaire have a higher increase rate (table 4). The urban concentration process will ease relatively slowly in Nigeria (tables 5, 6). While the large cities' development will be rapid in *T.A.*, compared to the world average, this increase rate has the tendency to decelerate.

Cities can also be understood as bigger or smaller nodes of population concentration spatially distributed on the country's territory. In *T.A.* it is a general phenomenon that the capital as primate city, instead of being centrally located in relation to its own country, is often a port oriented toward the colonial metropolis (Accra, Dar es Salaam, Kinshasa, Lagos, the latter being replaced by the new capital, Abuja/FCT, and Dar es Salaam by Dodoma.) This situation is detrimental to the country's infrastructure.

3. *Source of urban growth:* The main source of urban population growth in the developing countries is the natural population increase. In contrast, worldwide, the main source of the increase of the urbanization indicator (portion of people living in urban areas) as a structural change is rural-urban migration.

3.1. Decelerating rural-urban migration: Subjectively, migration is motivated by the perceived relative attractiveness of the cities and the countryside in terms of economic living conditions (income, subsidized social and public services; supplies in goods and their pricing) and of social living in general.

3.1.1. Population occupied in agriculture will further diminish in *T.A.* without necessarily diminishing agricultural production. Dynamic young people will leave subsistence farming as their main activity because of its low productivity. However, depopulation of rural areas can be prevented by promoting intensive cultures such as rice, and market-gardening (especially near the cities) which had a tradition notably in Western Africa. The policy promoting this goal includes financial means (for elementary mechanization), counselling (information about agrotechnique applicable in the tropics) and reorganization (more or less formal cooperatives based on local social tradition).

3.1.2. By definition, the urban area in contrast to the rural one has advantages in terms of cost-efficient development of convenient public services. For locating non-agricultural activities, urban areas also have the advantages of disposable manpower and access to markets. Instead of negating this basic fact by subsidizing unproductive industries, it is more reasonable to install some factories of limited size in rural areas where the labor force is cheaper and where natural resources may be available. The natural attractiveness of the countryside should be completed by basic public services (including public transport between localities).

3.1.3. Urban life-style includes physical facts (e.g., lighting for around the clock activities) and their perception. In reality, there are no architectural, urbanistic or societal means to cumulate the attractiveness of urban and rural living at the same place. Therefore, the potential immigrant should be informed about all aspects of the alternative living conditions between which he must choose. Presently, neither the urban immigrants' return visits to his native village nor the countries' mass media accomplish the task of giving a balanced image, the former because he protects his personal prestige and the second because it uses the metropolis as an important physical symbol of the fragile national unity. The concern for national unity is an understandable one for a young nation but it is paramount to prevent the metropole from becoming a showcase in the media.

3.2. Redirecting migration: Urban concentration creates specific problems in two respects. It increases congestion in the already overcrowded metropoles (e.g. shanties, lack of continuous electricity supply in Lagos) and it worsens the country's macrocephalic spatial disequilibrium by further development of the mostly peripherally located colonial metropolises (seaports). The issue of a sounder urban network can only be solved in the broader context of infrastructure (including communication, road networks, transport) of independent Africa on national, macro-regional, and continental levels.

3.2.1. The distribution of cities reflects a historical process everywhere (rivalries, hegemonies) and not planning based on economic calculation of optimal location. In order to actualize the new historical situation of decolonization by political, economic and social autonomy, $T.A.$'s countries should revive the African urban tradition (e.g., market towns). The actual African reconquest of the country, the well-conceived national unity as well as economic calculation point to the high-prioritied development of centrally located cities (when possible keeping African traditions alive). Instead of founding new cities, less developed countries should develop existing small cities (e.g., Bouaké in the Ivory Coast) involving fewer expenditures and better preserving African perspectives. (Sometimes an appropriate urban network can be designed by differentiating between administrative and economic metropoles.)

3.2.2. The promotion of centrally located cities will also diminish costly remigration from the center to the coast, and thus eventually produce a well-rooted (non-transient) African urban population.

3.2.3. No municipal or other urban policy conceived at a low administrative level and out of context of the country's societal policy can be effective. An Africa oriented urban network makes sense only if in a long-term perspective intracontinental (and intraregional) division of labor progresses, and if communication and road networks emerge along other routes than the colonial raw material export trade (staple), namely, East-West lines (instead of the direction of river or seaport or North-South caravan routes). The construction of these internal continental networks also contributes to mental decolonization and encourages Africans to give up the tendency to compare their own cities with those of the old metropolises such as London, Paris or Brussels. This kind of reconstruction can not be carried out without the initiative and coordination of the Organization of African Unity.

4. The urbanization process is not an isolated structrual change but an aspect of the societal and economic transition following independence in $T.A.$; therefore, the *underprvileged*'s situation in urban and rural settings

should be compared not only in quantitative but in qualitative terms, too. Furthermore, because of the differences in the various countries' colonial history and in their precolonial civilization (mode of production adapted to tropical forests or savannahs; the social system of extended family, matri- or patrilineal), the performance of social policy is better evaluated by time series than by international comparison.

4.1. In principle, quantitatively, the general level of income and its distribution (including differential use of subsidized public services) shows the means of subsistence at each social stratum's disposal. These data are rarely available with precision in countries with dual economy (*World Development Report:* 182–3; UN Economic Commission for Africa, *Survey,* 1980); therefore, the underprivileged's situation can be better assessed and monitored, policies' and special programs' performance better evaluated by societal indicators measuring consumption and its "human output": the physical and mental state of the targeted social stratum, while input data about production and income can be used for explanatory purposes (see figure on page 39).

4.1.1. On a global level, refined components of the Physical Quality of Life Index *(PQLI)* have the advantage that, targeted as policy goals, their improvement can be attained most efficiently when social policy effort is concentrated on the most underprivileged stratum of the society, which is a non-negligible advantage. However, despite its elegance as a formula, and its sensitivity toward the underprivileged, the *PQLI* itself cannot replace all other social indicators as an "end goal indicator". Considered at the technical level of measurement, infant mortality data are less reliable in *T.A.* than child death rate data; expectancy of an active life (including absence of morbidity) is not a less suitable indicator of well-being than life expectancy at age one; finally, new research shows that (elementary) schooling (including numeracy teaching) is more significant for the population's functional competency than the often disputable literacy data (e.g. in Liberia only 8% of Vai men were literate in English but 16% in Arabic and 20% in Vai script).

4.2. Because of qualitative changes in rural and urban life in a transitional society, the underprivileged's situation can only be observed by monitoring (in each setting) samples of subpopulations which are specifically exposed to negative discrimination in a particular neighborhood (uncontrolled settlements, etc.). Elderly and women are so-called minority categories. As we developed in this study, their situation within and outside the family is differently affected by rural-urban migration.

4.3. In so far as relevant data are available and reliable, life expectancy, infant mortality, child death rate and combined (primary and secondary) school enrollment are highly correlated and have a better showing in urban areas than in rural ones. These data disaggregated by sex also show a correlation for each sex, and can thus point to discrimination against women in particular countries.

5. Concerning the *supply* side, improvement in the underprivileged's situation results mainly from better public services, better housing and a more stable food supply. Particularly efficient are well-conceived special programs for non-working members of the population (such as *WIC*, viz. Women–Infant–Children) in predetermined high priority neighborhoods, providing they are fairly homogeneous.

5.1. With equal resource allocation, the public services in urban areas are better than in rural ones; however, basic services (e.g., access to potable water) should be provided at all points where residents must be maintained.

5.2. In rural areas, it is essential to assure a stable food supply by organization of food stocking and by development of the efficiency of the agriculture (cash crops and grain) which produces food for the farmers themselves and for the local market (versus intercontinental export market). This can chiefly be done by introduction of agrotechniques adapted to the tropics, guidance and cooperative reorganization.

5.3. Presently, quantitative assessment of the living conditions in the spontaneous settlements of the urban sprawls is rarely available. Shanties, etc. should be defined with more precision in function of tropical life-style (traditions of long periods of outdoor living; insulation, ventilation), and solutions researched while taking into account the differences between urban and rural living in terms of residential density as well as in terms of the development of family size and the size of other households in transitional *T.A.*

6. *Underemployment*: Besides natural resources such as tourism, oil and other mining products exploited by massive "Western" intervention of all kinds (often with neocolonial effects), the young jobless population is the most improtant resource for Africa's home-grown development; therefore, the development of labor-intensive technologies and sectors is a pivotal task. In the international context, in order to develop a genuine interdependent relationship with *T.A.* in mutual dignity, before any assistance, credit facilities and investment with easily repatriable profit, OECD Countries should first assure duty free entry for all African products (including manufactured ones (cf. UNCTAD).

6.1. During worldwide high unemployment as a general circumstance, the opportunity for any productive activity should be welcomed. While systematic, continuous and regular work is a fundamental characteristic of the industrial discipline, especially in transitional societies the residual sector, called also informal or non-structured, permits a country to keep in circulation a portion of its labor force whose active working time would otherwise be permanently lost. The spontaneous character of this sector is its vital condition. If the public authority cannot help these small businesses with financial assistance (often a loan of some thousand dollars suffices to give a new momentum to a household business) or free counseling (calculating, bookeeping, etc.), at least it should avoid harassing them with overregulations or discrimination against them because of their unsightly presence on the metropole's streets.

6.2. The residual sector's significance should be assessed in light of two main considerations:

6.2.1. The suppression of this low-income sector would leave to its earners the alternatives either of pottering around on the subsistence farm or of accepting the status of a begger or a passive recipient of public assistance.

6.2.2. The policing of this mushrooming sector should distinguish the productive branch (repair, etc.) which fills gaps in the national economy and serves as a place of apprenticeship for unskilled workers from the parasitic middlemen (who spoil the price system) accompanied by profiteers of illicit activities such as child prostitution and drug smuggling.

6.3. Producers for the market or for their own households, *T.A.*'s assertive and inventive young population should be sustained in their drive for a productive and active life. All initiatives for home improvement by do-it-yourself, etc. should be favored by legislative measures (e.g., protection of property rights of residents improving their homes), encouragement and advice from social organizations.

7. *Collective self-help:* while young adults have high individual mobility and the family household is no longer the main productive (and educative) unit, the kinship groups do not sufficiently assure the net of solidarity ties necessary for the redistribution of income to the non-earners.

7.1. Even though the government may be the last resort for the needy, it is still not in its interests to make more people than necessary dependent upon passive reception of public assistance. In order to allow the functioning of collective self-help, room should be left for multiple social institutions, formal and informal, which fill the gap created between the government and the nuclear family or even the single households.

7.2. If profit-making corporations took over the social functions of non-profit organizations in a paternalistic manner, it would not only distort the firms' competitive economic functions but also hinder the enfranchised citizen's emancipation and necessary mobility.

7.3. The government should especially assure cities free room for associations of any kind compatible with the common good: traditional ethnic-based groups, sibling-based peer groups, church organizations, neighborhood cooperatives, trade unions and other voluntary associations (mutal benefit societies, friendly societies, credit associations, etc.).

8. *Further studies and data collecting:* African countries have various historical backgrounds (which hindered Nkrumah's pan-african design), and they are in transition at different paces (cf. urbanization); therefore, *T.A.'s* development is badly served by sweeping generalizations based either on results extrapolated from isolated case studies or on ideological a prioris.

8.1. In transitional societies, an important substantive area for sample survey is the study of development of social networks (communication networks and structures) in relation to geographical and social mobility. Longitudinal (time series) studies carred out with appropriate sampling show the basis of actual solidarity ties (traditional and modern) in order to make effective experimental social programs. Research hypotheses should especially consider the coexistence and interaction of social formations of urbanized industrial society and those of the traditional kinship-based one, as well as social formations of a hybrid nature. Research design should allow qualifications of results by gross parameters such as the intergenerational diachronic aspects (urban in-migrants of first, second, etc. generations), ethnic groups (matri- or patrilineal) in the case of interethnic marriage in various circumstances (e.g., persistence of ethnic ties in function of internal or international migration). While for action-oriented research, time series are more important than synchronic international comparisons, it could be very useful and time-saving if universities of different countries coordinate their research especially in methodology by bilateral, regional or continental exchange (Association of African Universities).

8.2.1. Household survey: The household as an income sharing unit (involving mostly co-residence) is pivotal in the compound's and neighborhood's life and necessary to the latter's sociological handling. For planners, policy makers and evaluators, it is necessary to have a sampling scheme and the machinery to carry out household surveys concerning relevant aspects of the household's state (demographic characteristics and living conditions) and activity pattern (e.g., productive activities, time budgeting in high rise buildings compared to other neighborhoods). Thus, it is suitable that more African countries join the *National Household Survey Capability Program* (NHSCP) of the UN Statistical Office in collaboration with the UN Economic Commission for Africa. For developing this capability, there are 12 African countries who submitted proposals for donor countries but in *T.A.* Kenya is the only large country who did.

8.2.2. Monitoring units: Especially if a country has experimental social programs in progress, for operational reasons, it is indispensable to establish monitoring units which could periodically collect relevant data. In this respect, covering rural areas is a delicate and urgent task where the FAO's experience in data collecting can be helpful.

8.3. Census and basic data: In the course of this study, we have been obligated to reserve our conclusions because of the sparse and non-comprehensive data availability, as well as the irreliability[3] (lack of quality control at the data collecting site), discontinuity and irregularity in the data collecting for longitudinal studies. While survey data gathering is costly and time consuming, in the case of budgetary constraint, priority should be given to uniform, continuous and regular collection of basic census data with the possibility of disaggregation into *Small Areas Statistics (SAS)* in all countries in *T.A.* To make informed decisions it is paramount to update statistics and to estimate their reliability.

8.4.1. Continental Clearinghouse for African Data (*CAD*): The lack of continuity in African data often results from the dependence of multiple donors and ad hoc assistance. In order to optimize the decision-making process at all levels of Africa's public life (continental, regional, state, municipal), it is urgent that the OAU establish a continental *CAD* (cf. Pan-African Documentation and Information, – PADIS). The "clearinghouse" character of the data bank assures that a large budget would not be necessary, while mandatory contributions from all member countries could provide continuous and autonomous functioning.

8.4.2. The *CAD* catalogues existing data from the social field, makes them accessible and comparable by putting them in an epistemologically appropriate format which allows their qualification according to their probable reliability and generalizability. The *CAD* should attempt to be comprehensive and updated for available data. It should have the capability to inventory all sources (OECD: *Inventory of Data Sources*) of census, survey or case study data gathered and stocked by international, etc. organizations' data banks or elsewhere in more peripheral institutions' files. The created data transparency has the effect, on the one hand, to prevent redundancy and useless duplications, and on the other hand, to encourage new data gathering by showing the lack of specific data.

8.4.3. Concerning the data gathering itself, the *CAD* works as a coordinating institution in collaboration with the national statistical offices on standardization of data collection by using categories which are especially appropriate to describe African reality (e.g., tropical rural housing, food-types).

NOTES

1. We included neither Ethiopia (28 million inhabitants) nor Sudan (18) in this list because of their geographical and ethnic particularities. Even though the Ivory Coast and Uganda would replace Kenya and Tanzania in the list of *T.A.*'s major countries in terms of their global economic power *(GDP)*, we did not consider them because in urbanization studies population size is of paramount importance.

2. Cities with at least one million inhabitants.

3. *T.A.* lacks much basic data in general and collection with regular periodicity in particular (see also the UNRISD data bank). In international samples dealing with the source of urban growth, household size, sex and age distribution, occupational characteristics of rural and urban population, Tropical African countries are poorly represented or not at all (*UN Patterns:* 108, tables 11, 12, 24, 39). Infant mortality and income distribution statistics are especially scarce (*World Development Report:* tables 21, 25). The reliability of rural data has often been questioned (Casley; Scott) as well as statistics about uncontrolled settlements. But even in urban statistics the discrepancies revealed by consistency checks are high (e.g., over 30% discrepancy in Industrial Production statistics about value-added in Zambia; Fry in *UN Manual VIII:* 985). Rather than attributing low or high reliability to specific data (e.g., low reliability of literacy statistics), it is more important to know the marge of error with some precision. On the other hand, it is unjustified to consider statistics from developing countries as systematically less reliable. UN statistical publications abound in so-called printing errors, — happily some are obvious (e.g. According to *UN World Statistics in Brief* 1981: 14, Chad's GDP per capita in 1979 was $2188, Columbia's population in 1979 would be 10.92 million, while in 1970 it was 20.53 millions; and Turkey's and Spain's urbanization indicators until 1970 inclusive also are obviously wrong, cf. table 50 with tables 48 and 49 in *UN Patterns...* and *World Development Report:* table 20). The World Bank has apparently confused Zaire's urbanization indicator for 1980 with data from 1975 (cf. *World Development Report:* table 20 with *UN Patterns:* table 50)

BIBLIOGRAPHY AND DATA SOURCES FOR STUDYING TROPICAL URBAN AFRICA

For scientists Africa remains somewhat "the continent of discoveries". Compared to other continents, we dispose of relatively few reliable data which would allow systematic comparisons in space and time. This lack of data is reflected symptomatically in the studies themselves. J. J. Sprengler, for example, uses more USA data than African data hin is *Africa and the Theory of Optimum City Size* (in Miner: 55—89). On the other hand, we find that most authors, – even among Africans – instead of referring to a large sampling, draw their references from a narrowly based and deep but local knowledge of Tropical Africa. This is the reason that we were especially concerned with the problem of sources.

The special literature about Africa cities is larger in the English than in the French language. English research began nearly half a century ago, while the French research commenced systematically only in the 1960s (Mercier 398). Another problem is that Western Africa is better documented than other parts of Tropical Africa (Pons 529). S Amin, a specialist of the development of the Islamic savannah region, edited with J. W. Gregory a bilingual volume about migration in Western Africa, as a result of a symposium held in 1972; therefore, its data base can not touch the very significant last fifteen years of these independent countries.

Issues discussed also bear the sign of specialists who considered the subject first: geographers (J. Desch, J. Richard-Molard, D. Whittesley) and anthropologists (such as R. L. Beals). Anthropologists often look at urban Africa with a certain bucolic bias, nostalgic for their lost subject of study: rural African community. This was also an acceptable perspective for the colonial powers who considered black Africans in the city as a transient marginal population with permanent residences elsewhere (cf. "homeland" in the Republic of South Africa).

Another common pitfall is a strong ideological bias; Africa becomes a pure illustration of the imperialism theory, and consequently data and interpretation are intertwined. R. Sanbrook of Toronto did fieldwork in Ghana and Kenya and wrote a book about the *Urban Aspects of Assaulting Poverty in Africa,* considering eight countries. While his nearly fifty pages of footnotes are rich in bibliographical references, unfortunately his statistical data base is weak, somewhat "aged" and sometimes unreliable (p. 40). On the other hand, he is interested in nearly all African metropolises, but as a kind of "future Petersburg" (pp. 24-5), a power basis for revolutionary class struggle.

The Colloque International about *La croissance urbaine en Afrique Noire et à Madagascar* held in Talence/Bordeau between Sept. 29 and Oct. 2, 1970 was a breakthrough. It reunited some of the most important specialists and in its scope was very comprehensive. Many subsequent meetings and publications of the Study Center for Tropical Geography of Bordeaux are relevant for African urban issues and are included in our bibliography. The special issues of *Cahiers d'études africaines* about *Villes africaines* edited by Mercier (1973: 395–625) and *Villes africaines au microscope* (1981) are worth special mention.

It is unfortunate that not all communications to panels at the annual meetings of the USA African Studies Association are published, since many communications are relevant to our subject.

For census data the most important source is the *UN Patterns of Urban and Rural Population Growth* (New York City, 1980) and for specific data *Human Settlements in Africa: The Role of Housing and Building* edited by the UN Economic Commission for Africa (Addis Ababa, 1976).

* * *

Abu-Lughod, J. and R. Hay eds.
  1980 *Third World Urbanization.* London
Adedeji A. and L. Rowland
  1979 *Management Problems of Rapid Urbanization in Nigeria.* Ile-Ife
Agunbiade, S. A. and al.
  1979 *Urban Growth and Economic Development in the Sahel.* Washington, D.C.
Akare, Th.
  1981 *The Slums.* London
Altimir, O. and J. Sourouille
  1980 *Measuring Levels of Living in Latin America: An Overview of Main Problems.* Washington, D.C.
Amey, A.
  1976 *Urban-rural Relations in Tanzania.* Dar es Salaam
Amin, S. ed.
  1974 *Modern Migration in Western Africa.* Oxford
Amselle, J. L. et al. eds.
  1976 *Les migrations africaines.* Paris

Andorka, R.
1980 Long-Term Development of Hungary Measured by Social Indicators, in *Social Indicators Research* (8): 1–13

Ankerl, G.
1984 Sururbanisation dans le tiers-monde? in *Futuribles*, 25–48
1983 Traditional Construction and the Immediate Improvement of Tropical Africa's Housing Conditions in the Urban Sprawls, in *Actes des séances de L'Académie Royale des Sciences*, Brussels, 77–99
1983a Rapid Urbanization in the Third World with Special Reference to Tropical Africa: Social Impact and Perspectives, in *Labour and Society*, 277–288
1983b. What Makes the Present Economic Trend Critical and Economic Policy to Criticism in the OECD-Coutries? in *INU Forum:* 82. 06. 01—07.
1982 Migration From Rural to Urban Habitat in Tropical Africa, in *Mondes en Développement* (40), 511–534
1981 *Experimental Sociology of Architecture* (Paperback 1983) New York
1980. *Toward a Social Contract on a World-wide Scale*. Research Series No. 47. ILO, Geneva
1978 *Beyond Monopoly Capitalism and Monopoly Socialism: Distributive Justice in a Competitive Society*. Cambridge MA
1974 Specifische Faktoren in stadtsoziologischen Analysen, in *Kölner Zeitschrift für Soziologie*, 569–82
1973 Sociologie de l'espace, thème de l'architecture, in *Architecture, mouvement et continuité*, 83–42
1972 *Sociologues allemands: Etudes de cas en sociologie historique et non-historique avec le dictionnaire de "l'Ethique protestante et l'esprit du capitalisme" de Max Weber*. Paris-Neuchâtel
1971 L'environnement total et ses architectes, in *Architecture Concept*, 1–10
1965 *L'Epanouissement de l'homme dans les perspectives de la politique économique: Concept de l'investissement humain comme aspect de la politique de répartition*. Paris

Aryee, G.
1977 *Small-scale Manufacturing Activities: A Study of the Interrelationships between Formal and Informal Sectors in Kumasi*. Geneva

Bairoch, P.
1985 *De Jéricho à Mexico*. Paris. 80–92, 528–36
1977 *Taille des villes, conditions de vie et développement économique*. Paris
1972 *Le chômage urbain dans les pays en voie de développment*, Geneva

Balandier, G.
1968 *Dictionnaire des civilisations africaines*. Paris

Barbedette, L. and al.
 1975 La formation comme action sur la ville, in *Environnement Africain*, 1 (3): 19–54
Barnes, S. T.
 1977 Political Transition in Urban Africa, in *The Annals of the AAPSS*, (432): 26–41
Bascom, W. R.
 1962 Some Aspects of Yoruba Urbanism, in *American Anthropologist*, 64, 699–709
Basta S. S.
 1977 Nutrition and health in low income urban areas of the Third World, in *Ecology of Food and Nutriton:* 113–24
Beling W and G. O. Totten eds.
 1970 *Developing Nations – Quest for a Model*. New York City.
Bernard, G.
 1973 L'Africain et la ville, in *Cahiers d'Etudes Africaines:* 3
Berry, B. J. L. ed.
 1976 *Urbanization and Counterurbanization*. Beverly Hills, CA
Bogue, D. J.
 1969 *Principles of Demography*. New York City
Biniakounou, P.
 1977 *Chômeur à Brazzaville*. Dakar
Boserup, E.
 1970 *Women's Role in Economic Development*. New York City
Bromley, R. ed.
 1979 *The Urban Informal Sector: Critical Perspectives on Employment and Housing Policies*. Oxford
Bromley, R. and Ch. Gerry
 1979 *Casual Work and Poverty in Third World Cities*. Chichester, UK.
Bukh, J. and K. Ewusi
 Ghana, in *Measurement and Analysis of Progress at the Local Level*. 1978 vol. II: 1–85. UNRISD, Geneva
Bugnicourt, J.
 1976 Quelle alternative urbaine pour l'Afrique? in *Environnement Africain*, 2 (3): 3–22
 1971 *Disparités régionales et aménagement du territoire en Afrique*. Paris
Burundi. Ministère des travaux publics.
 1980 *Projet de développement urbain du Burundi*. Bujumbura
Byerlee, D.
 1974 Rural-urban Migration in Africa: Theory, Policy and Research Implication, in *International Migration Review*. 8 (4). Winter, 543–66
Le Cadre économique et démographique d'Abidjan à l'horizon 1985, in
 1979 *Revue Economique et Financière Ivoirienne,* (9): 4–11

Caldwell, J. C.
 1969 *African Rural-urban Migrations: The Movement to Ghana's Towns.* Canberra–NYC
Carley, M.
 1981 *Social Measurement and Social Indicators: Issues of Policy and Theory.* London
Casley, D. J. and Lury, D. A.
 1981 *Data Collection in Developing Countries.* Oxford
Chemain, R.
 1981 *La ville dans le roman africain.* Paris
Chenery, H. et al. eds.
 1974 *Redistribution with Growth.* Oxford
Clarke, J. I. and L. A. Kosinski eds.
 1982 *Redistribution of Population in Africa.* London
Cohen, M. A.
 1974 *Urban Policy and Political Conflict in Africa: A Study of Ivory Coast.* Chicago
Cole, J. P.
 1981 *The Development Gap: A Spatial Analysis of World Poverty and Equality.* New York City
Comhaire-Sylvain, S.
 1968 *Femmes de Kinshasa.* Paris
Cooper, F. ed.
 1983 *Struggle for the City: Migrant Labor, Capital and the State in the Urban Africa.* Beverly Hills, CA
Cotten, A. M. and Y. Marguerat
 1976 and 1977 Deux réseaux urbains africains: Cameroun et Côte-d'Ivoire, in *Les Cahiers d'Outre–Mer.* Oct. and Dec.
La croissance périphérique des villes du tiers monde: Le rôle de la promotion foncière et immobilière.
 1980 Talence–Paris
La croissance urbaine en Afrique Noire et à Madagascar.
 1972 Talence–Paris (Referred as *Croissance*)
Davidson, B.
 1959 *The Lost Cities of Africa.* Boston
Davis, K. and H. Hertz Golden
 1954 Urbanization and the Development of Preindustrial Areas, in *Economic Development and Cultural Change,* 6–24
Drewnowski, J.
 1970 *Studies in Measurement of Levels of Living and Welfare.* UNRISD, Geneva
Dubresson, A.
 1979 *L' espace Dakar-Rufisque en devenir: De l'héritage urbain à la croissance industrielle.* Paris

Durand-Lasserve, A. et al.
  1980 *La croissance urbaine dans les pays tropicaux: Croissance périphérique des villes: cas de Bangkok et de Brazzaville.* Talence–Bordeaux

Eckert, H.
  1978 Environnement infra-urbain des grandes villes africaines: pourquoi? in *Tiers Monde,* 19 (73): 149–59

Edwards, J.
  1975 Social Indicators, Urban Deprivation and Positive Discrimination, in *Journal of Social Policy:* 275–87.

Ela, J.-M.
  1983 *La ville en Afrique Noire.* Paris

El-Shakhs, S. and H. Amirahmadi
  1986 Urbanization and Spatial Development in Africa, in *African Urban Quarterly.* Jan.: 3–19

Eui-Young Yu
  1974 Components of Population Growth in Urban Areas of Korea 1960–1970, in *Population and Family Planning in the Republic of Korea.* Vol. II: 490–511.

FAO
  1979 *Production Yearbook.* Rome

Fapohunda, O. J.
  1980 Urbanization and Employment in Developing Countries: the Role of the Informal Sector, in *Labour and Society,* Jan.

Fassassi, M. A.
  1978 *L'architecture en Afrique Noire.* Paris

Fathy, H.
  1973 *Architecture for the Poor.* Chicago

Fei, J. C. H. and G. Ranis
  1964 *Development of the Labor Surplus Economy: Theory and Policy.* Homewood, IL

Fisher, L. F.
  1972 *Black Africa: A Comparative Handbook.* New York City

Fox, K.
  1974 *Social Indicators and Social Theory: Elements of an Operational System.* Chichester, UK

Friedman, J.
  1973 *Urbanization, Planning and National Development,* Beverly Hills, CA

Friedman, Y.
  1973 The Quarternary Sector, *UN University Program: Goals, Processes and Indicators of Development.* No. 18. Tokyo

Friedmann, J. and Th. Lackington
  1967 Hyperurbanization and National Development in Chili: Some Hypotheses, in *Urban Affairs Quarterly* (2) June: 3–29

Freund, B.
1983 *The Making of Contemporary Africa: The Development of African Society Since 1800.* Bloomington, IN
Giacottino, J. C.
1979 La ville tropicale et ses problèmes d'environnement, in *Cahiers d'Outre-Mer* (32): 22–38
Gilbert, A. and J. Gugler
1982 *Cities, Poverty and Development: Urbanization in the Third World.* Oxford
Ginneken, van Wouten
1976 *Rural and Urban Income Inequality.* Geneva
Glatzer, W.
1981 International Actors in Social Indicators Research, in *Social Indicators Newsletter,* August
Granotier, B.
1980 *La planète des bidonvilles: Perspectives de l'exploration urbaine dans le tiers monde.* Paris
Granovetter, M
1984 Small is Bountiful, in *American Sociological Review,* 3(49) : 323–34
Grove, D. and L. Huszár
1964 *The Towns of Ghana.* Accra
Gregory, Joel W.
See Amin
Gugler, J.
1982 Overurbanization Reconsidered, in *Economic Development and Cultural Change.* (31) 1: 173–89
Gugler, J. and W. Flanagan
1978 *Urbanization and Social Change in West Africa.* London
Gutkind, P. C. W. and P. Waterman eds.
1977 *African Social Studies: A Radical Reader.* New York City
Gutkind, P. C. W. and I. Wallerstein eds.
1976 *The Political Economy of Contemporary Africa.* London
Habitat, urbanisme, architecture en Afrique.
1972 in *Jeune Afrique.* July
Hake, A.
1977 *African Metropolis: Nairobi's Self-Help City.* London
Hance, W. A.
1970 *Population, Migration, and Urbanization in Africa.* New York City
Hanna, W. and J. Hanna
1971 *Urban Dynamics in Black Africa.* Chicago
Harris, J. R. and M. P. Todaro
1970 Migration, Unemployment and Development: A Two Sector

Analysis, in *American Economic Review*. March: 126-42
Harvey, M. E.
 1975 Interregional Migration Studies in Tropical Africa, in (L. A. Kosinski et al. eds); *People on Move*. London. 151-163
Hasse, de J.
 1965 *Le rôle des associations de ressortissants à Léopoldville*. Leuven
Hayuma, A. M.
 1979 Training Programme for the Improvement of Slums and Squatter Areas in Tanzania, in *Habitat International*. 4 (1-2): 119-29
Herbert, J. D.
 1979 *Urban Development in the Third World: Policy Guidelines*. New York City
Hjort, A.
 1979 *Savanna Towns: Rural Ties and Urban Opportunities in Northern Kenya*. Stockholm
Holland, P. W. and S. Leinhardt eds.
 1979 *Perspectives on Social Network Research*. New York City
Horwitz, M.
 1981 L'Afrique face à l'explosion urbaine, in *Croissance des Jeunes Nations*. (224) Jan.
Hoselitz, B. F.
 1953 The Role of Cities in the Economic Growth of Underdeveloped Countries, in *Journal of Political Economy*. Febr.-Dec.: 195-208
Hull, R. W.
 1976 *African Cities and Towns before the European Conquest*. New York City.
Hutton, J. ed.
 1972 *Urban Challenge in East Africa*. Nairobi
ILO *Employment, Income and Equality: A Strategy for Increasing Employment in Kenya*.
 1972 Geneva
ILO *Labor Force Estimates and Projects 1950-2000* Vol. V. World
 1977 Survey, Geneva
Jacolin, P. et al.
 1976 Actors and Social Forces: Dynamics of Change in an Urban Ward of Dakar, in *Environnement Africain*. 2 (1-2): 20-36
Jefferson, M.
 1939 The Law of Primate City, in *Geographical Review*. 226-32
Joshi, H. et al.
 1976 *Abidjan: Urban Development and Employment in the Ivory Coast* Geneva
Julien, Ch. et al. eds.
 1970 *Les africains*. T. III. Paris

Jules-Rosette, B.
1978 Alternative Urban Adaptations: Zambian Cottage Industries as Source of Social and Economic Innovation, in *Human Organization* 38 (3): 225–38
Juster, F. Th. and K. C. Land eds.
1981 *Social Accounting Systems.* New York City
Kaverschen, D. R.
1969 Further Analysis of Overurbanization, in *Economic Development and Cultural Change,* 2 (17), Jan.: 235–53.
Kayode, F.
1978 *Urbanization and Nigerian Economic Development,* Ibadan
Kebschull, H. G. ed.
1968 *Politics in Transitional Societies.* New York City
Kileff, C.
1972 African Views of Urban Life, in *Zambesia,* 2 (2)
King, A. D.
1976 *Colonial Urban Development: Culture, Power and Environment.* London
Konrád, Gy. and I. Szelényi
1974 Social Conflicts of Underurbanization, in (A. Brown et al. eds.) *Urban and Social Economics in Market and Planned Economies: Policy Planning and Development.* New York City
Kulikowski, R.
1980 *A Normative Model of Rural-urban Development and Optimal Migration.* Vienna
Kuper, H. ed.
1965 *Urbanization and Migration in West Africa.* Berkeley CA
Kuznets, S.
1972 Problems in Comparing Recent Growth Rates for Developed and Less Developed Areas, in *Economic Development and Cultural Change,* Jan: 185–209
Lacoste, Y.
1965 *Géographie du sous-développement.* Paris
Lagos Plan of Action for the Economic Development of Africa, 1980–2000.
1981 Geneva
Lake, L. A.
1978 Débats sur le thème: quel avenir pour la ville de Dakar? in *Notes Africaines,* (157) Jan.: 20–2
Laslette, P. ed.
1972 *Household and Family in Past Time.* Cambridge UK
Lawless, P.
1979 *Urban Deprivation and Government Initiative.* London
Ledent, J.
1980 *Comparative Dynamics of 3 Demographic Models of Urbanization.* Vienna

Lee, E. S.
1966 A Theory of Migration in *Demography*, 1
Les politiques urbaines en Afrique Noire.
1985 in *Politique Africaine*. No. 17, mars.
Lewis, W. A.
1954 Economic Development with Limited Supplies of Labour, in *The Manchester School of Economic and Social Studies*, (22) May: 139-91
1978 *The Evolution of the International Economic Order*. Princeton NJ
Linn, J. F.
1982 The Cost of Urbanization in Developing Countries, in *Economic Development and Cultural Change*, (30) April: 625-48
Lipton, M.
1977 Why Poor People Stay Poor: A Study of Urban Bias, in *World Development*. London
Lisk, F. and R. von der Hoeven
1979 Measurement and Interpretation of Poverty in Sierra Leone, in *International Labour Review*, 6
Little, K.
1974 *Urbanization as a Social Process: An Essay on Movement and Change in Contemporary Africa*. Boston
1965 *West African Urbanization: A Study of Voluntary Associations in Social Change*. Cambridge UK
Lloyd, P. C.
1977 *Power and Independence: Urban African's Perception of Social Inequality*. London
Lombard, J.
1954 Cotonou: Ville Africaine, in *Bulletin de l'Institut Français d'Afrique Noire*. 3-4
Mabogunje, A. L.
1977 The Urban Situation in Nigeria, in (Goldstein et al. eds); *Patterns of Urbanization*. Dalhousie. 569-641.
McGranahan, D. et al.
1979 *Methodological Problems in Selection and Analysis of Socioeconomic Development Indicators*. UNRISD, Geneva
McNulty, M. L.
1976 *West African Urbanization* in B. J. L. Berry
Meillassoux, C.
1978 *Urbanization of an African Community: Voluntary Associations in Bamako*. London
Mercier, P.
1973 Quelques remarques sur le développement des études urbaines, in *Cahiers d'Etudes Africaines*, 3

Methodological Problems in East Africa. Vol. III
 1969 5th Annual Conference, Dec. 8–12. Nairobi, Mimeo.
Michel, A. et al. eds.
 1981 *Femmes et multinationales.* Paris
Migration, Urbanization, and Third World Development, in
 1982 *Economic Development and Cultural Change.* Special Issue, 4
Mills, Cadman A.
 1980 *On Social Indicators and Development.* Project on Goals, Processes and Indicators of Development. (GPID). UN University, Geneva
Miner, H. ed.
 1967 *The City in Modern Africa.* London.
Mitchell, J.C. ed.
 1969 *Social Networks in Urban Situations: Analyses of Personal Relationships in Central African Towns.* Manchester
Moore, W. E.
 1963 *Man, Time and Society.* New York City
Morris, D.
 1979 *Measuring the Condition of the World's Poor: The Physical Quality of Life Index.* New York City
Morrison M. K. C. and P. C. W. Gutkind eds.
 1982 *Housing the Urban Poor in Africa.* Syracuse, NY
Mottin–Sylla, M.–H.
 1980 Solidarité des jeunes et des adultes pour la défense et l'aménagement du quartier, in *Environnement Africain* 4 (2–4): 189–200
Mushi, S. S.
 1980 *Institutionalization of Popular Participation: The Tanzanian Experience.* Paris, UNESCO
N'dione, E. S.
 1978 *La représentation de la ville chez les jeunes ruraux de Faudene, Sénégal: Analyse d'une série de romans-photos africains.* Lyon
Nelson, J. M.
 1979 *Access to Power: Politics and the Urban Poor in Developing Nations.* Princeton, N. J.
Newland, K.
 1980 *City Limits: Emerging Constraints on Urban Growth.* Worldwatch Paper, 38. Washington D. C.
Obudho, R. A. and S. El–Shakhs eds.
 1979 *Development of Urban Systems in Africa.* New York City
OECD
 1979 *Measuring Social Well-being: A Progress Report on the Development of Social Indicators.* Paris
 1979 *Inventory of Data Sources for Social Indicators.* Paris
O'Connor, A. M.
 1983 *The African City.* London.

Ofer, Gur
1976 Industrial Structure, Urbanization and the Growth Strategy of Socialist Countries, in *Quarterly Journal of Economics,* May: 219–44
Okediji, Q. O.
1975 On Voluntary Associations as Adaptive Mechanism in West African Urbanization: Another Perspective, in *African Urban Notes,* Series B: 51–73
Okpala, Don C. I.
1978 Urban Ecology and Residential Location Theories: Application in Nigeria's Socio-Cultural Milieu, in *Socioeconomic Planning Sciences,* 12 (4): 177–83
Osmont, A.
1978 *Une communauté en ville africaine: Les castors de Dakar.* Grenoble
Paige, E. and J. M. Paige
1981 *The Politics of Reproductive Ritual.* Berkeley CA
Pain, M.
1979 *Kinshasa: Ecologie et organisation urbaine.* Toulouse
1984 *Kinshasa: La ville et la cité.* Paris.
Paulme, D.
1953 *Les civilisations africaines.* Paris
Peel, J. D. Y.
1980 Urbanization and Urban History in West Africa, in *Journal of African History,* 21: 269–77
1982 *Cities and Sururbs: Urban Life in West Africa.* New York City
Peil, M. and Pius O. Sada
1984 *African Urban Society.* New York City
Perevedentsev, V. I.
1970 Migratsiia Naselen iia i Ispol'zovanie Trudovykh Resursov, in *Voprosy Ekonomiki.* Moscow, 34–43
Planification socio-urbaine et participation des plus pauvres,
1982 in *Les Carnets de l'Enfance,* 57/58
Pons, V.
1980 Urban Problems in Developing Countries, in *Third World Quarterly:* July
Potts, D.
1984 The Development of Malawi's New Capital Lilongwe: *A* Comparison with Other New African Capitals, in *Comparative Urban Research,* 10.
Rawls, J.
1978 *A Theory of Justice.* Cambridge MA
Raymaekers, P.
1963 *L'organisation des zones de squattering.* Léopoldville
Reimann, H.
1980 *Malta-Projekt.* Vol. I. Augsburg. Mimeo

Riddell, J. B.
1980 Is Continuing Urbanization Possible in West Africa? in *African Studies Review*, 23 (1)

Rihani, M. and J. Joy
1978 *Development as Women Matter: Third World Focus (An Annotated Bibliography)*. Washington D. C.

Roberts, B. R.
1978 *Cities of Peasants: The Political Economy of Urbanization in the Third World*. London

Roberts, B. W. G.
1980 The Capital Costs of Urban Development, in *Third World Planning Review*, (2) 1: 26–55

Rogers, E. M. and D. L. Kincaid
1980 *Communication Networks: Toward a New Paradigm for Research*. New York City

Rossi, R. J. and K. J. Gilmartin
1980 *The Handbook of Social Indicators: Sources, Characteristics, and Analysis*. New York City

Richardson, H. W.
1980 An Urban Development Strategy for Kenya, in *The Journal of Developing Areas*, 15 (1): 97–118

Rosette, B. J.
1981 *Symbols of Change: Urban Transition in a Zambian Community*. Norwood, N. J.

Sanchez, P. A. and S. W. Buol
1975 Soils of the Tropics and the World Food Crisis, in *Science*, Food Special Issue, May 9: 598–603

Sanbrook, R.
1982 *The Politics of Basic Needs: Urban Aspects of Assaulting Poverty in Africa*. London

Schmolder, K. and H. Hielscher
1966 *Nigeria: Von der tradionellen Gemeinschaft zur angepassten Sozialpolitik*. Stuttgart

Schwertfeger, F. W.
1982 *Traditional Housing in African Cities: A Comparative Study of Houses in Zaria, Ibadan and Marrakesh*. New York City

Scott, W.
1981 *Concepts, Definitions and Methods of Measuring Poverty*. UNRISD, Geneva

Schumacher, E. F.
1978 *Small is Beautiful*. New York City

Scribner, S. and M. Cole
1981 *The Psychology of Literacy*. Cambridge, MA

Seers, D.
1970 The Political Economy of National Accounting, in (Cairncross, A. and M. Puri eds;) *Employment, Income Distribution and Development Strategy: Problems of the Developing Countries.* New York City
Senghor, S. L.
1958 Cultura noire, in *Preuves,* Apr.: 36–7
Sheldon, E. B. and R. Parke
1975 Social Indicators, in *Science,* May 16: 693–9
Simon, D.
1984 Contemporary Decolonialization and Comparative Urban Research in Southern Africa, in *Comparative Urban Research,* 10.
Sjoberg, G.
1960 *The Preindustrial City: Past and Present.* Glencoe, IL
Soja, E.
1976 *Spatial Inequality in Africa.* Los Angeles, CA
Sovani, N. V.
1964 The Analysis of "Over-Urbanization", in *Economic Development and Cultural Change,* (12) 2, Jan.: 113–22
Southall, Aidan ed.
1979 Small Urban Centres in African Rural Development in *Africa,* 3 (49): 213–328.
Southall, A.
1976 From Segmentary Lineage to Ethnic Association, in (Owusu, M. ed.); *Colonialism and Change.* The Hague
Subramanian, M.
1970 An Operational Measure of Urban Concentration, in *Economic Development and Cultural Change,* 10.
Sylla, L.
1977 *Tribalisme et parti unique en Afrique Noire: Esquisse d'une théorie générale de l'intégration nationale.* Paris
Symposium on Social Indicator Research in an Urban Context.
1973 Ottawa
Szentes, T.
1975 *La structure de la société et ses mutations dans les pays africains.* Budapest
Tévoédjrè, A.
1981 L'interpellation, in *Les Universités Africaines rendent hommage à Felix Houphouët–Boigny.* Geneva, 31–58.
1980 Rapport final in *Quelle Afrique en l'an 2000?* Geneva, 9–32
1976 *For a Contract of Solidarity.* Geneva
Thandani, V.
1978/1979 Women in Nairobi: The Paradox of Urban Progress, in *African Urban Studies,* 2:67–87

Third World Urbanization, A Symposium,
  1982 in *Economic Development and Cultural Change* 3 (30) Apr.
Tobin, J. and N. Nordhous
  1978 Is Growth Obsolate? in (Moss and Milton eds); *The Measurement of Economic Growth and Social Performance*. New York City
Todaro, P. M.
  1969 A Model of Labor Migration and Urban Employment in the Less Developed Countries, in *American Economic Review*. March: 138–48
  1976 *Internal Migration in Developing Countries*. Geneva
UN
  1985 *World Population Trends, Population and Development Interrelation and Population Policies.* vol I, New York City
  1980 *Progress Report on National and International Work on Social Indicators*. New York City
  1979 *Patterns of Urban and Rural Population Growth*. ST/EA/Series S/68. No. 68. New York City (Referred as *UN Patterns*)
  1974 *Manual VIII: Methods for Projections of Urban and Rural Population*. ST/ESA/Series A/55. 74. XIII. 3. New York City
  1969 *Growth of the World's Urban and Rural Population, 1920–2000*. E. 1969. XIII. 3: 7–10, New York City
  1949 *The Main Types and Causes of Discrimination*. Lake Success, NY
UN Economic Commission for Africa
  1981 *Population Dynamics: Fertility and Mortality in Africa*. Addis Ababa.
  1980 *Social Conditions in Africa*. Part I (1978–9). Addis Ababa
  1979 *Household Data Requirements*. Addis Ababa (E/CN.14/SM/22)
  1978 *Demographic Handbook for Africa*. Addis Ababa
  1976 *Human Settlements in Africa: The Role of Housing and Building*. Addis Ababa
UNESCO
  1976 *Socio-economic Indicators of Levels of Living and Welfare*. Paris
  1956 *Social Implication of Industrialization and Urbanization in Africa South of Sahara*. Paris
Urbanization and Nigerian Economic Development
  1977 Proceedings of the 1977 Annual Conference. Nigerian Economic Society, Ibadan
Vennetier, P.
  1976 *Les villes d'Afrique Tropicale*. Paris
Verhaegen, B.
  1966 *Rebellions au Congo I*. Brussels
Villes africaines au microscope,
  1981 in *Cahiers d'Etudes Africaines*. 8

Vining, R.
1955 A Description of Certain Spatial Aspects of Economic System, in *Economic Development and Cultural Change:* 147–95

Wallerstein, I. and C. W. Gutkind eds.
1977 *Political Economy of Contemporary Africa.* London

Ward, P. M. ed.
1982 *Self-Help Housing: A Critique.* London

Ware, H.
1978 *Population and Development in Africa South of the Sahara.* Mexico City

Warren, D. J.
1981 *Helping Networks: How People Cope with Problems in the Urban Community.* Notre Dame, IN

White, H. C. and S. A. Boorman
1976 Social Structure from Multiple Network I–II, in *American Journal of Sociology,* Jan. and May

Willer, D. and B. Anderson
1981 *Coercion: The Elementary Theory and its Applications.* New York City

World Bank
1981 *Accelerated Development in Sub-Saharan Africa: An Agenda for Action.* Washington, D.C.

World Bank Atlas
1980 Washington D.C.

World Development Report
1981 Washington D.C.

Zapf, W.
1980 The SPES Social Indicators System in Comparative Perspective, in (Szalai, A. and F. M. Andrews eds.); *The Quality of Life.* Beverly Hills, CA

Zipf, G. K.
1949 *Human Behavior and the Principle of Least Effort.* Cambridge MA,

COMPLETE REFERENCE MAPS
HISTORICAL CITIES OF TROPICAL AFRICA

1 Abeokuta, Nigeria
2 Abomey, Benin
3 Accra, Ghana
4 Adulis, Ethiopia
5 Agades, Niger
6 Anomabu, Ghana
7 Awdaghost, Mauritania
8 Axim, Ghana
9 Axum, Ethiopia
10 Badagri, Nigeria
11 Bagamoyo, Tanzania
12 Bamako, Mali
13 Banjul, Senegambia
14 Bauchi, Nigeria
15 Benguela, Angola
16 Benin City, Nigeria
17 Birni-n-Kebbi, Nigeria
18 Bobo-Dioulasso, Burkina Faso
19 Bonduku, Ivory Coast
20 Bonga, Ethiopia
21 Bonny, Nigeria
22 Brass, Nigeria
23 Bussa, Nigeria
24 Calabar (Old), Nigeria

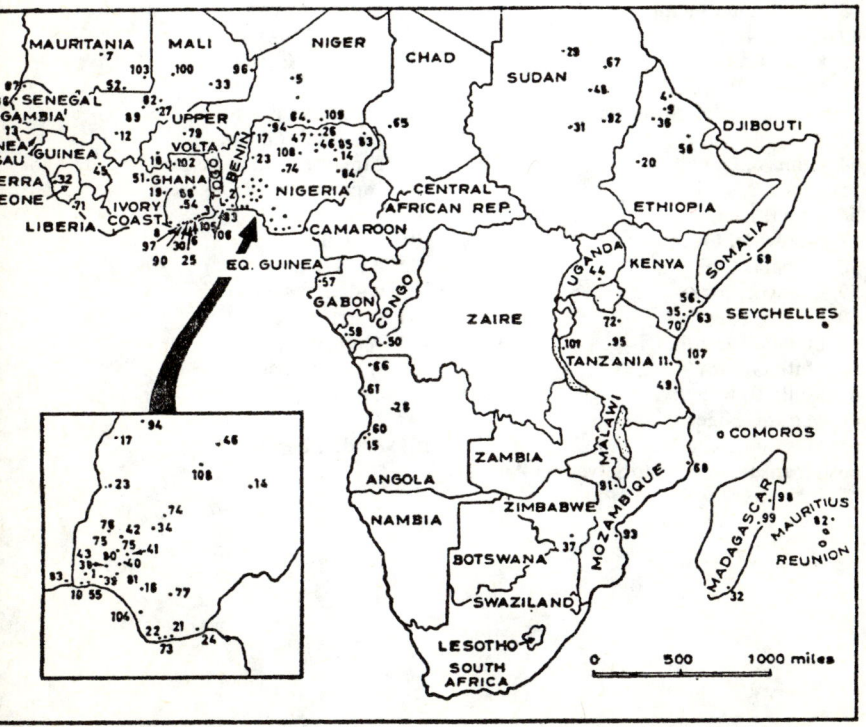

25 Cape Coast, Ghana
26 Daura, Nigeria
27 Djenne, Mali
28 Dongo, Angola
29 Dongola, Sudan
30 Elmina, Ghana
31 El Obeid, Sudan
32 Freetown, Sierra Leone
32 Taolanaro (Fort-Dauphin), Madagascar
33 Gao, Mali
34 Gbara, Nigeria
35 Gedi, Kenya
36 Gondar, Ethiopia
37 Great Zimbabwe, Zimbabwe
38 Ibadan, Nigeria
39 Ijebu-Ode, Nigeria
40 Ile-Ife, Nigeria
41 Ilesha, Nigeria
42 Ilorin, Nigeria
43 Iseyin, Nigeria
44 Kampala, Uganda
45 Kankan, Guinea
46 Kano, Nigeria
47 Katsina, Nigeria
48 Khartoum, Sudan
49 Kilwa, Tanzania
50 Kinshasa, Zaire
51 Kong, Ivory Coast
52 Koumbi-Saleh, Mauritania
53 Kuka, Nigeria
54 Kumasi, Ghana
55 Lagos, Nigeria
56 Lamu, Kenya
57 Libreville, Gabon
58 Lilibala, Ethiopia
59 Loango, Congo
60 Lobito, Angola
61 Luanda, Angola
62 Mali, Guinea
63 Malindi, Kenya
64 Maradi, Niger
65 Massenya, Chad
66 Mbanza-Congo (Sao Salvador), Angola
67 Meroe, Sudan
68 Mocambique, Mozambique
69 Mogadishu, Somalia
70 Mombasa, Kenya
71 Monrovia, Liberia
72 Mwanza, Tanzania
73 New Calabar, Nigeria
74 Nufi, Nigeria
75 Ogbomosho, Nigeria
76 Old Oyo, Nigeria
77 Onitsha, Nigeria
78 Oshogbo, Nigeria
79 Ouagadougou, Burkina Faso
80 Oyo, Nigeria
81 Owo, Nigeria
82 Port Louis, Mauritius
83 Porto Novo, Benin
84 Puje, Nigeria
85 Rano, Nigeria
86 Rufisque, Senegabia
87 St. Louis, Senegambia
88 Salaga, Ghana
89 Segou, Mali
90 Sekondi, Ghana
91 Sena, Mozambique
92 Sennar, Sudan
93 Sofala, Mozambique
94 Sokoto, Nigeria
95 Tabora, Tanzania
96 Tademekka, Mali
97 Takoradi, Ghana
98 Tamatave, Madagascar
99 Tananarive, Madagascar
100 Timbuktu, Mali
101 Ujiji, Tanzania
102 Wa, Ghana
103 Walata, Mauritania
104 Warri, Nigeria
105 Winneba, Ghana
106 Whydah, Benin
107 Zanzibar, Tanzania
108 Zaria (Zazzau), Nigeria
109 Zinder, Niger

OTHER CITIES OF TROPICAL AFRICA

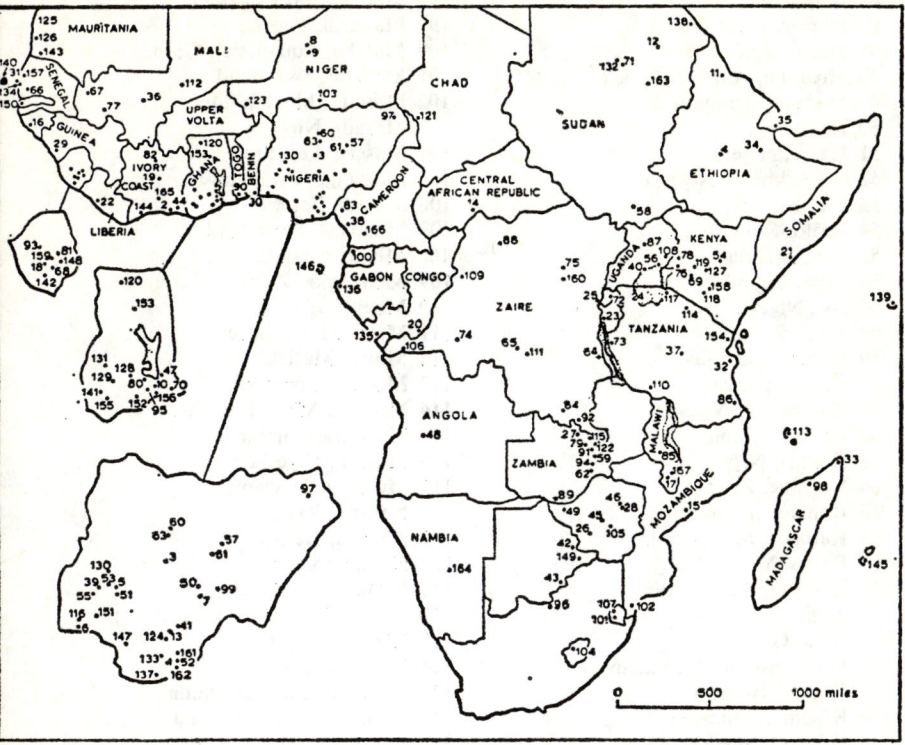

1 Aba, Nigeria
2 Abidjan, Ivory Coast
3 Abuja, Nigeria
4 Addis Ababa, Ethiopia
5 Ado-Ekiti, Nigeria
6 Ajegunle, Nigeria
7 Ajeokuta, Nigeria
8 Akokan, Niger
9 Arlit, Niger
10 Ashaiman, Ghana
11 Asmara, Ethiopia
12 Atbara, Sudan
13 Awka, Nigeria
14 Bangui, Central African Republic
15 Beira, Mozambique
16 Bissau, Guinea Bissau
17 Blantyre, Malawi
18 Bo, Sierra Leone
19 Bouaké, Ivory Coast
20 Brazzaville, Congo
21 Brava, Somalia
22 Buchanan, Liberia
23 Bujumbura, Burundi
24 Bukoba, Tanzania
25 Bukavu, Zaire
26 Bulawayo, Zimbabwe
27 Chigola, Zambia
28 Chitungwiza, Zimbabwe
29 Conakry, Guinea
30 Cotonou, Benin
31 Dakar, Senegambia
32 Dar es-Salaam, Tanzania
33 Diego-Suarez, Madagascar
34 Dire Dawa, Ethiopia
35 Djibouti
36 Djoliba, Mali
37 Dodoma, Tanzania
38 Douala, Cameroon
39 Ede, Nigeria
40 Entebbe, Uganda
41 Enugu, Nigeria
42 Francistown, Botswana

43 Gaborone, Botswana
44 Grand Bassam, Ivory Coast
45 Gwelo, Zimbabwe
46 Harare, Zimbabwe
47 Ho, Ghana
48 Huambo, Angola
49 Hwange, Zimbabwe
50 Idah, Nigeria
51 Ikerre, Nigeria
52 Ikot Ekpene, Nigeria
53 Illa, Nigeria
54 Isiolo, Kenya
55 Iwo, Nigeria
56 Jinja, Uganda
57 Jos, Nigeria
58 Juba, Sudan
59 Kabwe, Zambia
60 Kaduna, Nigeria
61 Kafanchan, Nigeria
62 Kafue, Zambia
63 Kakuri, Nigeria
64 Kalemie, Zaire
65 Kananga, Zaire
66 Kaolack, Senegambia
67 Kayes, Mali
68 Kenema, Sierra Leone
69 Kericho, Kenya
70 Keta, Ghana
71 Khartoum North, Sudan
72 Kigali, Rwanda
73 Kigoma, Tanzania
74 Kikwit, Zaire
75 Kisangani, Zaire
76 Kisumu, Kenya
77 Kita, Mali
78 Kitale, Kenya
79 Kitwe, Zambia
80 Koforidua, Ghana
81 Koidu, Sierra Leone
82 Korhogo, Ivory Coast
83 Kumba, Cameroon
84 Likasi, Zaire
85 Lilongwe, Malawi
86 Lindi, Tanzania
87 Lira, Uganda
88 Lisala, Zaire
89 Maramba (ex-Livingstone), Zambia
90 Lome, Togo
91 Luanshya, Zambia
92 Lubumbashi, Zaire
93 Lunsar, Sierra Leone
94 Lusaka, Zambia
95 Madina, Ghana
96 Mafeking, South Africa
97 Maiduguri, Nigeria
98 Majunga, Madagascar
99 Makurdi, Nigeria
100 Malabo, Equatosial. Guinea
101 Manzini, Swaziland
102 Maputo, Mozambique
103 Maradi, Niger
104 Maseru, Lesotho
105 Masvingo, Zimbabwe
106 Matadi, Zaire
107 Mbabane, Swaziland
108 Mbale, Uganda
109 Mbandaka, Zaire
110 Mbeya, Tanzania
111 Mbuji-Mayi, Zaire
112 Mopti, Mali
113 Moroni, Comoros
114 Mto Wa Mbu, Tanzania
115 Mufulira, Zambia
116 Mushin, Nigeria
117 Musoma, Tanzania
118 Nairobi, Kenya
119 Nakuru, Kenya
120 Navrongo, Ghana
121 N'Djamena, Chad
122 Ndola, Zambia
123 Niamey, Niger
124 Nnewi, Nigeria
125 Nouadhibou, Mauritania
126 Nouakchott, Mauritania
127 Nyeri, Kenya
128 Obo, Ghana
129 Obuasi, Ghana
130 Offa, Nigeria
131 Offinso, Ghana
132 Omdurman, Sudan
133 Owerri, Nigeria
134 Pikine, Senegambia
135 Pointe Noire, Congo
136 Port Gentil, Gabon
137 Port Harcourt, Nigeria
138 Port Sudan, Sudan
139 Port Victoria, Seychelles
140 Praia, Cape Verde
141 Prestea, Ghana
142 Pujehun, Sierra Leone
143 Rosso, Mauritania
144 San Pedro, Ivory Coast
145 Saint-Denis, Reunion
146 Sao Tome
147 Sapele, Nigeria
148 Segbwema, Sierra Leone

149 Selebi-Phikwe, Botswana
150 Serekunda, Senegambia
151 Shagamu, Nigeria
152 Swedru, Ghana
153 Tamale, Ghana
154 Tanga, Tanzania
155 Tarkwa, Ghana
156 Tema, Ghana
157 Thies, Senegambia
158 Thika, Kenya

159 Tongo, Sierra Leone
160 Ubundu, Zaire
161 Umuahia, Nigeria
162 Uyo, Nigeria
163 Wadi L-Madani, Sudan
164 Windhoek, Namibia
165 Yamoussoukro, Ivory Coast
166 Yaounde, Cameroon
167 Zomba, Malawi